U N B R O K E N

Jonny Hüttner in 1932

UNBROKEN

*Resistance and Survival
in the Concentration Camps*

LEN CROME

SCHOCKEN BOOKS
NEW YORK

First American Edition

Copyright © 1988 by Len Crome

Library of Congress Cataloging-in-Publication Data

Crome, Len.
  Unbroken: resistance and survival in the
concentration camps.

  Includes index.
  1. Hüttner, Jonny.   2. Rote Sprachrohr (Group)
3. World War, 1939-1945—Prisoners and prisons, German.
4. Political prisoners—Germany—Biography.   5. Communists—Germany—Biography.   I. Title.
D805.G5H873   1989   940.54'72'43   88-43061
ISBN 0-8052-4064-0
ISBN 0-8052-0881-X (pbk.)

Manufactured in the United States of America

Contents

Illustrations

Foreword

British authors who have written about German resistance to the Nazis frequently refer to the activities of such people as Carl Goerdeler, Claus von Stauffenberg, Martin Niemöller, Dietrich Bonhoeffer and Hans and Sophie Scholl of the Munich White Rose group. Many principled anti-fascists, whether Communist, Social Democrat or Christian, who opposed the Nazis throughout, have been ignored. The most numerous and consistent amongst them were the Communists. This is now broadly, if sometimes grudgingly, recognised. The first aim of this book is to tell the story of a group of young people – mostly, but not exclusively, Communists – who did all they could to resist the Nazis before and after their seizure of power in 1933.

It may help to define more closely at the very outset the term 'resistance' as used in the sub-title of this book. Some readers may interpret it as implying physical confrontation with the Nazis, but inside Germany this was virtually impossible and, with a few exceptions, never occurred. After 1933, resistance, always heroic and costing many lives, consisted mainly of clandestine political activity and propaganda, and the preservation of anti-Nazi political parties and organisations. In prisons and concentration camps resistance took the form of the common struggle for survival, mutual aid, occasional sabotage and the maintenance of morale and of the belief in ultimate liberation.

This book looks at resistance to the Nazis – and especially opposition within the concentration camp system – through the life of an individual, Jonny Hüttner, and his close friends and comrades in *Das Rote Sprachrohr*, one of the famous agitprop theatre companies which flourished in Germany before 1933. Part One follows Jonny Hüttner's life from childhood in a poor working-class neighbourhood in Berlin through to his escape from a concentration camp in 1945. Part Two follows the lives of some of the *Das Rote Sprachrohr* members under the Third Reich, while Part Three presents one of the few *Rotes Sprachrohr* scripts to survive and biographical information on members of the company.

In Part One Jonny Hüttner's own account is interleaved with historical material on the prisons and camps in which he spent the years from 1936 to 1945, supplemented with statements from other survivors from the concentration camps. The entire book has been read and approved of by Jonny Hüttner.

Before embarking on this work I wrote to the Central Committee of the Socialist Unity Party of the German Democratic Republic outlining my project and asking for their help. This was amply and generously given. I was able to interview and record on tape and paper the recollections of most of the people involved in the story who are still alive in the German Democratic Republic. I was also allowed to study the archives and files of the Gestapo and of the Nazi judicial and prison systems, and to use the library of the Institute of Marxism-Leninism. I was able to visit the relevant former concentration camps, and to follow physically Jonny's escape route. In addition, I was supplied with publications and books, most of which were otherwise unobtainable. For all this I am deeply grateful.

I am also grateful to the many survivors of the Nazi period who were kind enough to discuss their own experiences with me at length. I would like to thank Jonny Hüttner and our mutual friend Erich Mirek for placing their collections of photographs, some of which are reproduced below, at my disposal. Most of all, my thanks must go to Jonny Hüttner himself, without whose participation and sustained help the book could not have been written.

It gives me much pleasure to acknowledge the assistance I have also had in this country. My son, Peter, lent me his word processor, taught me to use it, and extricated me from the many traps into which I stumbled in the early stages of my operations. He also read the manuscript, making many useful comments, as did my wife Helen (Jonny's sister). I owe a great debt to the historian Allan Merson and his wife Betty, who read the text, commented usefully and encouraged me to go on with it and to seek publication. Merson's own book, *Communist Resistance in Nazi Germany* (London 1985), is a rich source of information on the subject and has been invaluable. The text has also been read by my Polish friends, Emilia and Hubert Meller, who helped me with their unrivalled knowledge of recent German and Polish history, and I was privileged to receive the assistance of the acknowledged German historian of the anti-Nazi movement, Luise Kraushaar. Professor Josef Schleifstein has likewise added a number of cogent observations. I am in debt to Nicholas Jacobs, whose expertise I greatly admire, for the initial editing of the text. The English version of Heinrich Heine's lines and poem used in the text is by Hal Draper.

Len Crome
November 1986

Prologue

Paris,
28 June 1945

My dearest sister,
Many times, again and again, I have to re-read your letter. It
grips me suddenly in the metro, at meals, in the middle of the
night, and I have to take it out and go over it once more. Our
past is reborn and you know how much I loved you! I am
specially glad that you have made me an uncle. Now I have a
nephew who will perhaps want to play with the hair around
the bald patch on my head. I would also like to meet and to
get to know my new brother-in-law.

Yes, Lenchen, now I can wipe the sweat off my brow, relax
and look back at the madness of the years that have passed
since we parted. It began to look ominous at the very start,
with the Gestapo, and later in the concentration camps not
much was needed to stop me from ever writing to you again.

So to make a start: after cycling home that evening from
the Seidels' flat, you will recall that it was 18 March 1936, I
was arrested in front of our house by six Gestapo men, and
after they also arrested you and Trude, was taken with Rudi
Seidel to Alex. [The Berlin police headquarters used at that
time as interrogation centre by the Gestapo, L.C.]

The interrogation started the following day and was
conducted with intimidation and torture. I had been heavily
incriminated by a prisoner who had broken down under
previous interrogation, and described me as a leader of
a dangerous group of intellectuals. The Gestapo knew almost
exactly how many members we had by the total amount of
dues that I collected and passed on. They also had some

particulars of our underground activity. I swore from the first moment not to reveal a single name or address to them. At times it was very hard to hold out and I was already close to suicide but I grew firmer and stronger day by day. After eight weeks the Gestapo abandoned their futile efforts. I was taken to the Moabit remand prison. The conditions there were bearable. In February 1937 I was sentenced to three and a half years of prison and four years of '*Ehrenverlust*' for the 'preparation of high treason'. [*Verlust der Ehrenrechte* translates as 'loss of honours' but there is no precise English equivalent; loss of civil rights comes closest to the real meaning. L.C.] I expected a more severe sentence. My Act of Indictment carried on conviction punishment ranging up to the death sentence.

I was taken to serve my sentence in the Brandenburg-Görden prison. There I shared a cell with two others and felt better after my long solitary confinement. The prison was full of political prisoners. We exchanged secret messages and shared news. My two cell mates were splendid comrades. Unfortunately they are no longer alive.

I was told three months before the end of my term that I would be handed over to the Gestapo and that meant concentration camp. A trying time ensued for me before I was actually released on 19 September 1939, and the freedom seemed quite unreal to me. It was only a bureaucratic mistake from which they quickly recovered. On arriving in Berlin I found no place to hide, was arrested within twenty-four hours and sent to Sachsenhausen.

When I saw what was happening there I did not think that I could possibly survive more than eight days. We were 260 people in a room 12 × 8 metres and had to lie all day on our stomachs, partly on top of each other. The windows were nailed down and the ventilator shaft plugged. Every few minutes the SS would enter and order us to do physical exercises. Those unable to carry on were beaten to death. When the brutes left, some of us, parched with thirst, dared to crawl up to the windows and lick the condensed moisture off the window panes. We had up to fifty deaths in the hut every day and new prisoners kept on arriving. This torture went on to the end of their Polish campaign in October. They then kept on discovering equally horrendous methods to torment us. In October 1941 they brutally murdered 12,000 Russian prisoners of war. In May 1942 they shot every third Jew in reprisal for the killing of Heydrich [a senior SS officer killed by the Czech resistance. L.C.].

In October 1942 all the remaining Jews were lined up and made ready for what we assumed to be our killing. I was one of eighteen prisoners taking part in a protest demonstration. We threw ourselves at and hit out at the SS in front of the 12,000 assembled prisoners on the barrack square. That event is my finest memory and I shall describe it in a future letter.

We were then transferred to Auschwitz, and after going through a 'selection', I was placed into a work-squad. Prisoners not gassed at once on arrival could expect to live on average no longer than three months. Conditions improved slightly later, especially for me, when I was made medical orderly in the camp sick-bay.

In January 1945, when the Soviet Army approached Auschwitz, we were evacuated to the Dora concentration camp in Thuringia. The journey in open coal trucks in severe frost lasted eight days and was one of my most terrible experiences. At least half the prisoners died from the frost, hunger and thirst.

In the Dora camp conditions were once again critical and I was threatened with transfer for extermination to the Bergen-Belsen camp. Fortunately, I was able to escape during an air-raid by the allied airforce.

Well, to continue! The first days in freedom I felt completely dazed, as if dreaming. Then, settling down, I could no longer feel elated. I was alone, had no one to rejoice with me. A longing seized me for my family, for friends. Were they alive? They murdered our mother in 1942. We must bear this heavy loss so common in the world today. She had always had to struggle desperately hard and suffered much on account of my imprisonment. I did not know if you were still alive. Now I know. You, Max and our sisters Rosa and Ada are alive and so is father.

With all my love,
Jonny

Jonny (Johann or Nathan Hüttner) wrote the above letter to Helen (Lenchen) who lived at the time with a friend and their children in a house near Semer in Suffolk. Both were waiting for their husbands to be demobilised.

Part One:
Jonny Hüttner

1
Childhood in Prenzlauer Berg

Jonny's parents came to Berlin singly in 1911 from their native Austrian towns; they met, married and had five children: Rosa, Jonny, Helen, Ada and Max.

Rapid growth of industry around the turn of the century had led to a great influx of workers needed in the factories and the service industries of Berlin. Cheaply built tenements, so-called *Mietskasernen*, sprang up over the eastern parts of the city; Prenzlauer Berg, situated directly north of Alexanderplatz – then one of the main working-class areas – was one of these. It was there, in the southern part of the district, that the new family found its homes, changing them several times in the course of the next twenty years.

The father was called up and served in the Austrian army during the First World War. The post-war years, when the children were growing up, were a time of hardship for many working people like the Hüttners. Unemployment and inflation impoverished them. They lived, then, seven of them, in a flat with one room and a kitchen. There was no electric light, the staircase stayed unlit, and one sometimes stumbled over drunken men. Prostitutes stood at the street corners.

The squalor and signs of poverty were, of course, not confined to the southern part of Prenzlauer Berg – all working-class districts were much the same. And only a short mile to the west there bubbled and sparkled another life, a world city displaying immense luxury: caviar from the Caspian, oysters from Normandy; champagne, cabarets and more intimate haunts, spectacular erotic musicals. There one could find beautiful women and willing boys – all that money can buy. It was later to become 'Isherwood's Berlin'. On the other hand, it was also one of the foremost European centres of culture, with superb music, splendid museums, avant-garde theatre, great schools of learning. All that was a scarcely accessible foreign land to the dwellers of the slums of Prenzlauer Berg, except the few who did menial jobs in the west.

Until 1986 some tenements in Prenzlauer Berg remained unreplaced. Second World War bombing demolished many of them, and squares have been made out of the open spaces that resulted. Many remaining buildings bore the scars of bomb splinters, shrapnel and the bullets used in the battle for the city in 1945. Large, rusty refuse boxes stood in the courtyards and the plaster of the walls and corridors was peeling. In 1987 the city celebrated its 750th anniversary and the authorities have cleared some of these slums.

Jonny Hüttner's father's employment was sporadic. He tried at times to support the family by selling stockings in the market but failed repeatedly and in the end abandoned the family. The mother did all she could but conditions overwhelmed her and she was forced to accept help from relatives, the Jewish community and other charities. The hardest blow fell when, unable to feed all her children, she was forced to place the two youngest, Max and Ada, in an orphanage.

Close to Diedenhofer Strasse, where the family lived until 1922, is the Kollwitz Strasse and the Kollwitz Platz, named after the famous artist Käthe Kollwitz who used to live there. Her husband, Dr Karl Kollwitz, looked after the young Hüttners from their earliest infancy. He was a general practitioner and treated children with special understanding and affection. He knew their first names and would stop and chat with them in the street. Many of his adult patients were not on the panel and he treated them all free.

The Kollwitzes occupied a second floor flat with the consulting-room on the first floor. One entered a long corridor with chairs standing by the wall for the waiting patients. Most were women, thin, drawn and pale. Many were pregnant. Käthe Kollwitz would come down, open the door, always calm, always in dark clothes. Her son had been killed in the First World War and she never got over the bereavement. She passed along the line of the waiting women, and very likely drew inspiration from them, using them as subjects for her pictures. The people of the district knew that she was a great artist and she is, of course, justly famous now. But her husband, a steadfast friend and protector of the poor, should also be remembered, as he is by the Hüttners.

Jonny was born on 21 November 1913 and faced at once and recurrently Prussian officialdom over the entries in his birth certificate. There was, to be sure, no difficulty over his first name – Nathan, nor over the gender – male, but the surname was a problem. The state did not fully accept religious marriages, like that of his paternal grandparents, which were not duly recorded in official Register Offices. They had been married according to the Jewish ritual, in that part of Poland which had been part of the Austro-Hungarian Empire. His grandfather's surname was Hüttner and the grandmother's Hirschtritt. After the First World War that part of the Habsburg Empire became Polish and so all children and grandchildren became Polish citizens, their official name being always written as 'Hirschtritt *genannt* Hüttner', i.e. alias Hüttner, although for all practical purposes they used the Hüttner surname, as did all their close relatives. Later, under the Nazis, when Jonny joined the underground resistance, he adopted the name of Jonny, short for Johann, so as not to endanger his non-Jewish comrades, any association of 'Aryans' with Jews being punishable. In prison and concentration camps he was again Nathan Hirschtritt, and it was only a few years after the liberation that he became at last and officially Johann Hüttner.

Jonny attended the primary school at Kolmarer Strasse where unluckily he had the same teacher for all the eight years of his schooling. Herr Bielicke had been an NCO during the war and was proverbially Prussian to the marrow of his bones. An ardent anti-Semite, the very sound of the name Nathan made him bristle. Bielicke disliked Jonny who was undernourished and the smallest in the class. Since the

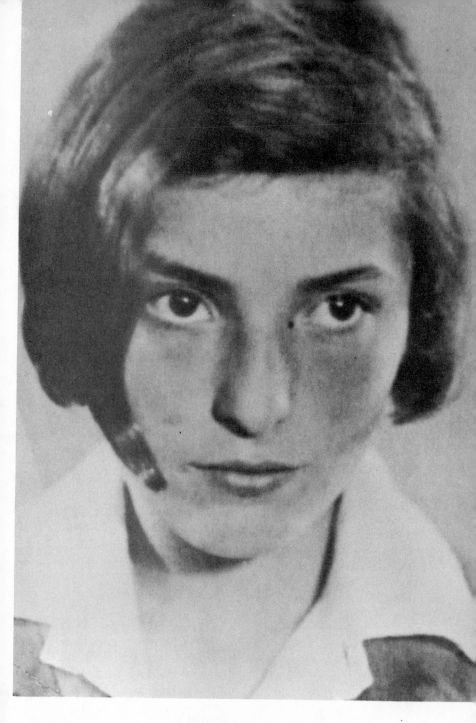

Helen Hüttner in 1932

teacher beat him the stronger boys did likewise, and so he learned early to be tough, to return blow for blow – until the others began to respect him.

Bielicke was not an exception; there were many such teachers in Germany. Prussian primary schools were like reformatories. The children had to sit with arms outstretched over their desks, were not allowed to to go out to relieve themselves during lessons and were punished at every opportunity. The Hüttners retain no happy memories whatever of their school days. Yet in spite of the schools and their poverty they were not unhappy. They loved each other and their mother, and did what they could to shield themselves from the hostile environment. For all the teacher's malevolence Jonny obtained a good leaving certificate and that was the end of his formal education.

Helen was only a year and a half younger than Jonny, and in the family they were always closest to each other, sharing the same friends and interests, and joining the same societies. Their two schools occupied the same building, though the girls' and boys' halves had different entrances. Even Jonny's chief tormentor had a double in Helen's class, Fraülein Janecke, just as senselessly cruel and anti-Semitic. Helen hated the school and was a bad pupil. Things, however, changed when she was twelve, with the arrival of an understanding new teacher who took an interest in Helen. She rapidly became one of the best pupils, so much so that she was advised to transfer to another school, one that prepared children for further education – a so-called *Aufbauschule*. The one proposed was the Karl Marx Schule in the Berlin district of Neukölln, and so an interview was arranged for her. This had to be done without the knowledge of Helen's mother, who needed all that her children could earn. She hoped that Helen would start work on leaving primary school at the age of fourteen, and was aware that the hope that her children might continue schooling was not realistic.

Helen was accepted. For the first time in her life she realised that school could be fun, and she was soon one of the most popular girls. The pupils were mainly children of progressive parents, and Helen's views were naturally influenced by her companions. Earlier, the anti-Semitism she had experienced inclined her towards Zionism; now she began to identify with workers and the unemployed. In 1929, when the traditional May Day demonstrations were forbidden by the police, barricades went up in Neukölln and she witnessed the shooting by the police which caused many casualties. She joined the *Roter Pfadfinder Bund* (Red Scouts) and almost at the same time the Young Communist League.

The teachers advised her to stay on at school, and promised to try and find some financial help, but she could not withstand the pressure of poverty at home and left at the age of sixteen to serve an apprenticeship in the office of an engineering factory. She was paid 30 marks a month the first year, and 40 marks the second year. Being young and pretty she was persistently molested by the superiors.

While still at school the children attended a day nursery (*Kinderhort*). It was a hospice for poor Jewish children who went there after school, which finished between twelve and one o'clock. They had dinner there and could stay till six in the evening playing and doing their homework. One of the women running the place, Frau Marjory Hellmann, was the wife of a director of the Diskonto Gesellschaft, an important German bank. She was an amateur artist and took a fancy to Jonny who showed an interest in painting. She wanted to help the Hüttner family and asked her husband to take him on as trainee at the bank.

And so, aged fourteen, Jonny started work at the bank in 1927. The chief of the department was told to help him in every way, and did so. Jonny's job was filing. His predecessor took four hours over it; after a little practice Jonny could do it in two. He was doing well enough but, like many others of his friends at that time, thought that the only honourable occupation was manual work, and so left the bank after a year. This was a terrible blow for his mother who had been very happy at the thought of her son's secure future. The bank did not approve of his plan either but nevertheless found him an apprenticeship with a firm of painters and decorators. The new work was hard and the wages, 3.50 marks a week, compared with the 60 marks a month he had been earning at the bank. Neither he nor the family were happy with the new work and, since his mother needed all the pfennigs that he could earn, he gave up the apprenticeship and took up unskilled work, becoming in turn messenger, office boy and transport worker. Much of the time he was unemployed and like thousands of others was drawn to the German Communist Party, which at that time took more interest in those out of work than any other party.

2

Das Rote Sprachrohr

The political turbulence of Germany in the 1920s was reflected in the cultural life of the country. Appreciating the danger hanging over Germany, many intellectuals, writers, artists, scientists and others working in the field of culture began to take a more active part in the left-wing movement. New ways were sought in art and culture. The theatre was opened to experiment and innovation by, for example, Erwin Piscator in Berlin. However, although many German theatres were subsidised, and thus more readily accessible than in some other countries, most workers could nevertheless scarcely afford to visit them. There also existed in Germany 'Workers' Theatres' influenced by the Social Democrats but largely apolitical in nature, with a central Workers' Theatre League, but these functioned by and large as amateur dramatic societies putting on plays of an overwhelmingly conventional nature. (In the late 1920s all agitprop troupes affiliated to the Workers' Theatre League and soon steered it in a more propagandist direction.)

Socialist and Communist propaganda was conducted, as it always had been, by speeches in halls, factories or in the open air, and of course by the printed word: newspapers, journals, pamphlets, leaflets and books. It was an uphill struggle against a well entrenched establishment: over half the media was controlled by one man – Alfred Hugenberg, a militarist and former director of the Krupp armament works. The situation therefore favoured the search for new ways of communication between the Communist Party and the workers. This was the background for the extraordinarily rapid spread of the agitprop movement between 1927 and 1932, a new form of propaganda expressing the aspirations of the workers and combining appeal for political action with full throated dramatic entertainment.

A stimulus in the formation of the first German companies was the visit in 1927 of one of the Soviet *Blaue Blusen* ('Blue Shirts') agitprop troupes, while another element of the shows – choruses, as in ancient Greek tragedies – had also been used in some plays and meetings. Very rapidly all the larger German cities acquired one or more agitprop companies. The leadership of the Communist Party realised the potential of this form of propaganda and gave it full support. The scale of the agitprop theatre movement was extremely impressive. In the four weeks preceding the 1930 Reichstag elections, for example, nineteen Berlin agitprop companies gave 650 performances in halls, courtyards, buildings, factories, in the open and in the countryside before 180,000 spectators. They recruited 1,200 new members to working-class organisations, sold party literature and made collections for the party election fund.

Some of the Berlin agitprop companies such as *Kolonne Links, Alarm* and *Roter Wedding* (named after the working-class neighbourhood Wedding), became well known, but *Das rote Sprachrohr* (Red Megaphone) was perhaps the most popular. Two special factors played a part in this troupe's success. Working mainly in Berlin, it collaborated directly with the propaganda department of the Central Committee of the Communist Party and performed at large demonstrations and meetings before or after the speeches of the party's leaders, like Ernst Thälmann or Ernst Schneller. Secondly, the *Rotes Sprachrohr* was fortunate in having as director a gifted and fiery young professional actor – Maxim Vallentin.

Maxim's father, Richard Vallentin, directed the first German production of Gorky's *Lower Depths* at Max Reinhardt's Kleines Theater on Berlin's Unter den Linden in January 1904. Maxim's mother, a dramatic actress, played Anna in the play and was pregnant at the time. When the child was born a few months later the choice of the first name for the newborn, Maxim, was wholly predictable, and he could later justly claim to have been on the stage even before being born.

His father died when Maxim was four years old and he was

brought up by his mother. He began conventional theatre training at the age of fifteen and a few years later was given his first parts. At the time it was difficult for young actors to obtain durable contracts and so he moved from cast to cast. While engaged in Piscator's historical pageant *Trotz Alledem* ('In Spite of It All') he made friends with a number of colleagues who like him were mostly unemployed, and did unpaid stage work with them at some Communist Party functions. A breakthrough came in pat theatrical fashion when an actress playing Oberon in *A Midsummer Night's Dream* fell ill and he had to take over her part the following day – to the Titania of Marlene Dietrich. At the age of twenty he married Edith Wolf, a dancer trained in the Mary Wigman school of modern ballet. Thereafter she proved a tower of strength to him in private and professional work and, later, in exile and political life. Gradually, both became frustrated by and disillusioned with the bourgeois theatre.

Still with no political affiliation, Maxim visited the Communist Party's headquarters and explained that as a man of the theatre he was interested in propaganda by artistic methods. The response of the interviewer, Hermann Duncker, the party's education expert, was somewhat disheartening: 'Teach the workers to appreciate the beauty of the Venus de Milo, they will then be better at making revolution.' A little later he was requested by the Secretary of the Young Communist League for the Wedding district, Franz Fischer, to organise and direct for it one of the yearly 'Three Ls' (Lenin – Liebknecht – Luxemburg) celebrations. Instead of using, as expected, a chorus, he wrote what he called, without further explanation, a *Kollektivreferat* (a collective address). A hundred young workers volunteered for the show – the first Young Communist League improvised agitprop cast.

The company's first proper show, initially performed in Hamburg, was *Hands off China*, its main theme being protest against the 1927 imperialist intervention in that country. They were then asked to go to a German-speaking frontier area of Czechoslovakia and support a miners' strike there. On returning Vallentin formed the permanent *Das rote Sprachrohr*. The second show, produced on the occasion of the Young Communist League Congress in 1928, was

Maxim Vallentin in 1930

Hallo, Kollege Jungarbeiter ('Hello, Young Worker'). It consisted of a sequence of scenes in the life of a young worker, following him through home, school, street and factory. It showed how the capitalist system robbed the young of their joy in life, impoverishing them and endangering their future by unemployment and preparations for war. The next programme was *10 Jahre Komintern* ('Ten Years of the Comintern'), which was so successful that in 1929 the troupe was invited to take it on tour to the USSR. What they experienced in the Soviet Union inspired the next and last of their full programmes, first performed in 1930, *Alles für die Sowjetmacht* ('All for Soviet Power'). This show lasted ninety minutes and consisted of three main parts. The first dealt with the civil war and the establishment of the Soviet state. The second demonstrated the profound changes in the daily life of the people, the elimination of illiteracy, the growth of culture and the Five Year Plan. The third was about the defence of the Soviet Union. (Part of the text is reproduced in the appendix on pp.168-70.)

In addition to these full programmes the *Rotes Sprachrohr* accumulated a stock of shorter or *ad hoc* pieces for special audiences, such as workers on strike, the unemployed and tenement dwellers, as well as shows directed against the eviction of non-payers of rent, and others to be performed in the open, in the countryside, and so on. Certain 'closed performances' inveighed against male Communists who were not treating their wives as equals – leaving them to domestic chores whilst they themselves attended meetings or just talked politics with their comrades over beer. Sketches shown to young people ridiculed exhibitionism in dress and speech.

Maxim Vallentin also tried to help less experienced troupes, invited their members to rehearsals and shows, and gave them at all times the benefit of his expertise. In 1928 the Communist Party and the Young Communist League started publishing a journal entitled *Rotes Sprachrohr* devoted to the theoretical and practical aspects of agitprop work. Maxim appointed Elli Schliesser as editor of the journal.

Elli Schliesser was born in 1911 in the Scheunenviertel, an area of Berlin inhabited by some of the poorest and most religious Jews. At the age of sixteen, passing an open

Erich Mirek in 1931

window, she saw the *Rotes Sprachrohr* at rehearsal inside. She stopped to watch and listen, returned the following day, and again the next. Maxim Vallentin noticed her and asked her to join the company. There is something awe-inspiring in Elli's subsequent development and rise to prominence in the agitprop movement. Being highly intelligent, she had also an insatiable thirst for knowledge and studied constantly. She was also a natural singer and banjo player. She had a talent for friendship and leadership, and her fellow members referred to her admiringly as 'Our Rosa' (meaning Rosa Luxemburg) or, more jokingly, as 'Karl Marx without a beard'. Maxim Vallentin would discuss all political issues affecting the company and its programmes with her. They would agree on a common standpoint, and in this way established a dual leadership – professional and political – of the company.

Elli not only edited *Das rote Sprachrohr* but also did much of the writing herself and was thus influencing the outlook of agitprop troupe members throughout Germany. In 1932, aged twenty-one, she was elected chair of the International Revolutionary Theatre League in Moscow.

Other members of the *Rotes Sprachrohr* included Rudolph Seidel, a Young Communist and office-worker, who had been a member of the Alarm troupe since 1928, and Gertrud Knopp, who came from a middle-class family, amongst whom there were a number of Nazis, in Aachen; Rudi and Trude were married in 1934.

Erich Mirek had joined the company after meeting the Vallentins in a Wilmersdorf bar. The Vallentins had asked Mirek about a fellow member of the Anti-Fascist Young Guards who had applied to join the *Rotes Sprachrohr* but unfortunately had a heavy stutter; Mirek had recently been impressed by *Ten Years of the Comintern* and ended up joining the troupe himself.

Helen Hüttner attended a meeting at which the *Rotes Sprachrohr* put on a sketch and their performance stunned her. Someone from the troupe noticed her and suggested that she come for an audition. She did – and was quite hopeless. Not only was she terrified and bad at acting but she thought that her appearance was all wrong: all the other girls in the troop moved with long assured strides, were rather strong and masculine, while she was petite, very feminine and walked – according to Maxim Vallentin – hopping like a bird. Yet her sincerity was convincing, and she was taken on.

Rehearsals began and were strenuous for her; she was one of the few who was employed, having to get up at seven in the morning, working till five in the afternoon, and then going to rehearsals, which often went on till midnight. She would often fall asleep at her boring work in the office. Life now centred around the troupe. She felt that she was learning, improving and making a political contribution. She was making new friends and also had her first serious and lasting love affair with another member, Erich Mirek.

Margarete, or Gretl, Berndt came from a Communist family in north Berlin and had been in a Communist children's group from the age of ten. A seasonal worker in a chocolate factory, she attended a party branch meeting in 1930 and was approached by Elli Schliesser and Maxim Vallentin who asked whether she would like to join the *Rotes Sprachrohr*. She had not seen that troupe in action but had seen some of the other agitprop companies, liked what she saw, and so readily agreed.

She was first taken to a conference of the agitprop troupes then being held in Leipzig and, after returning to Berlin, began intensive rehearsals. The company was preparing the *All for Soviet Power* show and lengthy rehearsals were held almost every day. Gretl happened to be in one of her periods of redundancy and so was able to attend all of them. She was very impressed with Maxim Vallentin's direction. He would not tell the actors how to speak their lines or how to move but asked them what they would themselves say in the circumstances, how they would say it and how they would move. Then, after discussion and agreement, the scene would be repeated endlessly until it became totally ingrained and automatic.

The play was soon ready and began to be performed all over Berlin. It was not always given as a whole. Thus during the engineering workers' strike in 1931 selected scenes were performed. Gretl also went on tour with the company to Saxony, Thuringia, the Rhineland, Saar and Ruhr. When they were on tour, local troupes would come to *Rotes Sprachrohr* performances. They would come again to rehearsals, join in, learn some of the company's songs and engage in lively discussion.

Gretl turned out to be a 'natural', acting with ease, in character and with full assurance. She was handsome, was and looked a working-class girl, and so was soon often photographed for illustrated journals. When Slatan Dudow was assembling his cast for Brecht's *Kuhle Wampe*, he wanted Gretl to take the principal part. Vallentin objected. He did not wany any individual members of the troupe to be picked out for a 'star' part. They were always to remain a team, acting and working together, and so they did. Gretl fully agreed although the offer was tempting. In the event, due to an accident she was unable to take part in the film even as a member of the team.

In 1932 a second team was formed which toured towns in western Germany for three months, and a third team organised children's shows. In 1931 some of the company had taken part – playing an agitprop company – in the film *Kuhle Wampe*.

Maxim Vallentin possessed a remarkable ability to translate political actuality onto the stage by unerringly finding the right words and action. He was also a highly talented teacher, getting people to work together, to respect one another. There were no cliques or rivalry in the company. Erich Mirek believes that it was thanks to this feeling of collectivity instilled and nurtured by Maxim Vallentin that no member of the *Rotes Sprachrohr* deserted the socialist cause, even in the darkest days of the Third Reich. All the members of the company retained total confidence in each other and did not panic when danger came.

More than half a century later, it is difficult to picture an agitprop company like the *Rotes Sprachrohr* at work in Germany before the Nazis came to power. One of the few accounts in existence is by Tucki Basse, whose husband, a documentary film-maker, worked with the troupe and made a short film which, unfortunately, does not survive.

'Basse was asked one day by his friends and his friends' friends to attend a rehearsal of a workers' theatre company. It took place at 9 o'clock in the evening in a north Berlin pub.

A small cheerless room, chairs and tables pushed aside to

the wall to leave space in the centre for the actors. Almost all were young workers, mostly unskilled or unemployed, splendid people with beautiful natural movements. They sat waiting by the wall in their colourless dark clothes and could scarcely be seen by the light of the dim lamp. They were softly fingering their instruments, each for himself, so as not to disturb the others. Mike, a handsome motor mechanic, of feline grace and shining eyes, rattled his drum. Erich, with a quiet Slav face, played the accordion. The dark Edith and the delicate Grete hummed softly, with surprisingly hoarse voices. Mary, a thin English girl in the corner, accompanied with a few chords on an old piano. Maxim stood in the centre discussing the new play with two comrades. Edith extracted from her briefcase a thermos, sandwiches for two, or more, and all the 'costumes' needed in the play.

Actually, the piece they were to rehearse was a very short one – only a few lines of text dealing with Russian peasants from *All for Soviet Power*. Each of the peasants was poor and slogged away at his inherited tiny plot. A soldier, with new ideas gathered in the city, passed by and called out, 'Tear down the old fences and build a collective farm. It shall be so, and for the best!' However, a reactionary kulak appears and wants to harm the collective. The peasants speak indignantly about it: 'Ein Kulak der wollt es wagen uns vergiften eine Kuh, – doch man kriegt ihn an den Kragen, schwups – hat ihn die GPU!' (A kulak has dared to poison our cow but we got him by the scruff of his neck, and, hey presto, he is in the hands of the GPU!')

It seemed so terribly naive. How would it sound on the stage? And the costumes? All retained their identical boiler suits changing only their headgear. The peasant women tied the ends of red headscarves under their chins; the soldier was given a dented grey top covering with a red star over a helmet, and the kulak wore a peaked cap. The props were a knee-high fence to be leaped over by the agile soldier and to be torn down later on his advice. There was also a leather flask with a clearly visible label 'poison' for the wicked kulak and, lastly, a small cardboard window with bars on it for him to hold in front of his face to indicate arrest and imprisonment by the GPU.

Parts were distributed.

'Edith can't speak loudly today. The doctor forbade it for a week.'

'Good. Then Elli will play the peasant's wife for the week.'

'Gerda, you will be the second peasant woman. But, please, brush your hair under the headscarf. You look like one of those UFA film girls with a kiss curl.'

'It's because I have no mirror,' retorts Gerda.

'Erich's helmet doesn't fit. It's because his head is too thick!'

'Then Erich will be the peasant and Mike will play the soldier.'

'But I am already playing the kulak.'

'Well, well, then you will play two parts and we'll give you double pay.'

There was of course no pay whatever. Members worked voluntarily – for the cause. Some had done an eight-hour day already before coming, and the ten pfennigs for the fare was also a problem. Maxim would help out. He kept a little cash to pay some fares and a few other modest expenses. Members were used to having no money.

The spirit of the troupe was splendid. Was it good human material, well chosen and attuned to each other? Or was it Maxim's gay and easy manner that made everything work? He was their chief – and hence their best comrade; or the reverse: best comrade – hence their chief. And young as he was he ran the show with complete assurance: to him it seemed like child's play. The texts were mainly by him – mostly verses with short pithy lines. He knew how to present the action in the simplest way with many original ideas – turning shortage to advantage. It all flowed smoothly, all of a piece. The five-minute scene of the peasants and kulak was spoken jointly in chorus or individually, and the spectator was not only fascinated by it but also fully convinced of its integrity.

A few songs for the next performance had to be gone over towards the end of the evening. The troupe lined up with their instruments, megaphones and drum. Mary struck a few encouraging chords on the piano and the singers started with a force reminiscent of the fall of Jericho. As they stamped their feet it sounded like a gun barrage. Fearing the collapse of the building Basse began to look round for the emergency exit. But nothing broke, and there were no complaining neighbours. On the contrary, Maxim shouted, 'Louder,

louder! Tomorrow you will have to take on 2,000 workers.'
He stamped his feet and shook his black curly head wildly,
and really managed to raise the crescendo to fortissimo. They
shouted with all their might; it was no longer singing but a
clearly articulated roar; one heard every word distinctly.
Heroic vocal chords! No wonder they kept on going to the
ear, nose and throat man for treatment, and could only talk
to each other in whispers.

At the end of the shattering war dance the spectators were
more exhausted than the singers. Now that the discipline of
the rehearsal was lifted the members became lively. They
exchanged jokes and daily events in a thick Berlin dialect,
often derisively, but without any coarseness or indecency of
speech. There was much warmth and mutual sympathy
between those fresh young people. Grete was a packer in a
sweet factory, Gerda a typist, Erich was unemployed and
helped his father – a greengrocer – Mary had just married a
bookseller who traded from a cart at one of the street
corners. She was expecting a child. Edith was Maxim's wife.'[1]

The activity of the agitprop companies began to attract
increasing attention from the authorities. Their performances often drew attacks by the Nazis and their supporters, and
could thus be a cause of public disorder, but this was perhaps
more of a pretext than a reason for true concern; the success
of the agitprop movement in its propaganda and recruitment
was probably alarming the government. Restraining
measures began to be taken against them in 1931 following a
circular to that effect issued by the Reich President's office.
In 1932 the Police President of Berlin – the Social Democrat
Grzesinsky – instructed his force to impede performances of
the troupe by direct prohibition or by imposing obstructive
conditions.

Scant attention was paid to the new obstacles by the *Rotes
Sprachrohr*. The company continued to appear as before but
would station pickets to warn them of the approach of the
police so as to escape, if necessary, through prearranged
exits. Even on the entry of the police the performance was
not always stopped.

It hardly needs saying that the politics of the *Rotes
Sprachrohr* was at all times faithfully that of the Communist

Party, whose declared aim was the establishment by revolutionary means of proletarian dictatorship and a Soviet Germany. Such a policy was, of course, totally unacceptable to the other great working-class party – the Social Democrats – without whose agreement and partnership the defence of the Weimar Republic, let alone a socialist revolution, was scarcely realistic. This was recognised ultimately at the Seventh Congress of the Communist International held in Moscow in 1935, and at the so-called 'Brussels Conference' of the German Communist Party, also held in Moscow, which followed it. Sectarianism was officially abandoned, but by that time the Nazis were in full control.

All members of the company were simultaneously members of the Young Communist League or, later, of the Communist Party, and so had additional responsibilities. Dues were paid and collected. Topical political issues were discussed regularly in relation to the preparation of texts and performances. In the intervals of the shows members of the cast would come down to mix with the spectators, invite them to join the party or associated organisations and sell pamphlets and newspapers. At some of the larger meetings up to forty new recruits could be enlisted. After courtyard performances they would run up the stairs of the tenements, knock at the doors, and offer propaganda material. One large factory in the city and one village would be adopted, i.e. come under the patronage of the troupe, who would visit them regularly, giving performances and establishing personal contacts. Occasionally, but rarely, the company would run a residential school on the theoretical aspects of Marxism-Leninism, where the tutors were often officials of the party's Central Committee.

Maxim Vallentin was a strict disciplinarian and also insisted on a high standard of moral conduct which had, of course, little in common with conventional bourgeois morality. Its main principles were tireless work in rehearsal and performance, loyalty, comradeship, devotion to the party and the troupe, and absolute honesty. Those who could not keep up with the high standard were excluded. It must also be said that members were so totally involved in the work of the company, especially if they were also employed, that they had virtually no time left over for other commitments and contacts. One

Members of *Das Rote Sprachrohr* at a youth hostel near Berlin in 1934; Jonny Hüttner is at the end on the right, with Erich Mirek next to him

result of this pressure was that relations – social, matrimonial or romantic – were almost entirely with other members of the company.

All open activity of the *Rotes Sprachrohr* ceased after the Nazis came to power in January 1933 but it continued to function as a party branch. In accordance with the party's directives, members joined various mass organisations so as not to be isolated and in order to influence as many people as possible. They joined in the first place amateur dramatic societies where they tried to persuade their colleagues to put on plays with a social content, usually classical ones by Kleist or Molière. Maxim also rehearsed Georg Büchner's *Wozzeck* with some of the members. Others joined sports organisations and ramblers' or choral societies. Jewish comrades also entered Jewish clubs as cover, such as the *Bar Kochba* sports club. Others, including Hüttner, joined the so-called *Werkleute*, an organisation formed for the training of young people in various crafts, other than agricultural, in preparation for emigration to Palestine; a few of these youngsters later joined the Herbert Baum resistance group. All continued to pay their party dues and received leaflets and other propaganda material which they tried to dispose of to some of the more trustworthy among their new colleagues. Outings were arranged to the outskirts of Berlin, places frequented by workers, especially the unemployed. There they sang, neutral songs first, and then specially composed ones with mild political content. They tried to provoke discussion among those listening to them.

Organisationally the troupe had split after January 1933, again in line with party policy, into small groups operating in three of the Berlin districts: Prenzlauer Berg, Pankow and Neukölln. Until contact with the party was re-established money collected as dues was given to the wife of Ernst Schneller. Contact was later maintained through the Neukölln district but that broke with the arrest of the district leadership. The last contact with the party was re-established in the summer of 1935 – with the district of Prenzlauer Berg – and ended in the arrest of four of its members in March 1936.

Notes

1. Tucki Basse's account is lodged in the State Film Archives of the German Democratic Republic; it has not been published before.

3

Politics and Arrest

66When out of work I began to stand with the other unemployed in front of the Karl Liebknecht House, the headquarters building of the German Communist Party. We formed small groups, I listened to the conversation and what I heard appealed to me. One day a young man with a Young Communist League badge on his lapel came up to me and asked if I would like to come to their branch meeting. I accepted and heard Rudi Arndt, a wonderful man.[1] His speech and the ensuing discussion won me over. So, in the spring of 1930 I joined the Young Communist League and was soon involved in street encounters with the Nazis.

On Sundays we conducted our 'house and courtyard propaganda'. One of us would speak in the yard, windows would open and people listened. We appealed particularly to the young, and after the speech would go up the stairs to try to sell our paper – *Die Junge Garde*. We were happy if we could dispose of about fifty copies.

On some Sundays we travelled to the country for what we called 'countryside action'. There our propaganda was conducted in market squares and in villages. Sometimes we would arrange small meetings. But in the country we were often harried by the police who attacked us with dogs.

We put up leaflets and posters on walls. Immediately after 30 January 1933, when Hitler became Chancellor, our leaflets called for a general strike. Very soon I was elected *Litmann* [literature secretary] for the branch, which meant that I had to fetch and distribute newspapers and booklets. Some of these I read but I did not receive any systematic Marxist training.

In 1932 I joined the agitprop troupe *Das rote Sprachrohr*. I don't really know how I became a member of the company. I think that it was my sister Helen, already a member, who suggested that I join and, of course, through her I had already met and knew some of the members. They needed someone to tune their instruments quickly and I could do that. I could play the guitar and also learned the accordion, which gave us stronger background sound.

My special assignment was work with the young workers of a branch of the I.G. Farben Industrie Gesellschaft, the largest German chemical trust. As a result of this work I went as delegate in July 1932 to the Anti-fascist Action Congress, for which about 1,000 participants assembled in the concert hall of the Berlin Philharmonic Society.

After the Nazis came to power we decided that it was not enough to be only *young* Communists, so all the members of the *Rotes Sprachrohr* joined the Communist Party as a group. We paid our dues and held regular meetings, usually outside Berlin – masquerading as ramblers. Later we split up in groups according to our place of residence. Only one of us collected dues for the whole of the *Rotes Sprachrohr*.

Until contact was established with our district the dues were used to support the wife of the imprisoned Ernst Schneller.[2] I was the dues collector for the twenty remaining members of the company. Our own group had four members, the other three being Rudi Seidel, his wife Gertrud and my sister Helen. When at last we found contact with the Prenzlauer Berg district, it was through a man named Liermann (this was his real name but at the time we only knew him as 'Walter'). I would hand over all the collected dues to him and receive propaganda material from him.

On 18 March 1936 we held a meeting of our group in the Seidels' flat. We knew that there had been arrests in the district and thought it necessary to suspend our activity. That the flat was used as a meeting place was known also to Liermann. After a short time the bell rang and Rudi went to the door. He returned looking worried. Liermann, he said, had been at the door and asked whether I was by chance at the flat. Rudi denied this. Liermann then told him that there had been arrests and that all twenty members from whom I collected dues were to be called urgently to a meeting in order to elect a new leadership. Rudi, who became suspicious, replied that he did not know the others and that Liermann had better find me; he himself did not know where I was.

We considered all this and decided that Liermann would probably go to my home; he knew my address. I was to cycle there at once to try and forestall him, to stop him from entering our flat and speaking to mother, who knew nothing of our illegal work. And I was to tell him that our group was dissolved and that we wanted no further contact. When I got there Liermann was to my surprise already standing outside the house. As soon as I approached him we were surrounded by men in plain clothes. One turned to me, not to Liermann: 'Are you so and so? Your papers!' I asked for his warrant and he pointed to the criminal police badge on his lapel. They then took me to the local police station and locked me in a metal-lined closet [*Blechkasten*]. What happened to the others I discovered later.

After locking me up the police proceeded to the Seidels' flat and there arrested my sister and Gertrud Seidel. Rudi Seidel was not in; he had left at once after my departure to cycle down to Neukölln to warn the comrades there. He had all his personal documents on him, thinking of escaping abroad, but could not leave his wife alone and decided to go home first; he was arrested in front of his house.

Soon after midnight I was taken out of my cell and pushed into a car where I found Rudi. Both of us were taken to the police headquarters at Alexanderplatz. In the reception cell there we were able to whisper to each other that we were only having coffee and engaged in no political conversation. It was agreed that Rudi Seidel would maintain that he knew nothing of the purpose of our get-together; he was merely letting us use his flat. Then I was taken to a single cell. The interrogation started the following morning.

Liermann knew the address of the Seidels' flat because he came to a meeting there with representatives of the groups of the *Rotes Sprachrohr* living also in parts of Berlin other than Prenzlauer Berg. As a measure of security he was not told their names nor did he know that they were all members of the *Rotes Sprachrohr*. Had the Gestapo found out they would have arrested the lot.

The interrogation on the 19 March was conducted by four Gestapo men. At first I said nothing but they confronted me with Liermann who admitted receiving dues from me for twenty members and supplying leaflets and propaganda coins. (Superficially these looked like real coins but carried an anti-Nazi inscription and a simple picture, such as a smashed swastika.) This I had to confirm. My story was that I knew only the first names of the people whose dues I collected and that I never knew their addresses. Since as Jews we were not allowed to associate with 'Aryans' the names I invented had to be Jewish, like Israel, Daniel, and so on. And I said that they they had all gone abroad.

The Gestapo did not believe me. On the third day they said that to save myself a lot of pain I was to tell them at once the names and addresses of the people. As a foretaste they gave me two powerful blows with a rubber truncheon on my backside. Then they made me face the wall in a half knee-bent position, not too high and not too low, and kicked my swollen buttocks with their boots. After about half an hour I was ordered to get up.

They threatened me with four further blows with the truncheon, followed by another six, then eight and so on, with knee-bent sessions between the beatings. I could be spared if I gave them the names. I stuck to my story and was dealt four blows and then more and more. After each blow I would tip over and if not up quick enough would be kicked with their boots on my soft parts. And again: 'The names.' Once more the knee-bent posture, giving me a chance, they said 'to think it over', and further beatings. By late evening they were exhausted and ordered me to take down my trousers. On seeing my enormously swollen buttocks they declared *Feierabend* [closing time] and left saying, 'To be continued tomorrow.'

That night I dreaded facing them again the following day. I was also afraid that driven mad by pain I would give away the names. I began to look round for a way to kill myself. In one corner I saw some glass fragments with which to cut my artery at the wrist. At the seam of the drainage pipe high above the lavatory pan I could attach a rope and hang myself. I tore into the sheet on the bunk. Yes, it could be done! With the noose round my neck I could deal myself a blow over the head with the heavy cover of the lavatory. Those were my thoughts. Then they changed. Let the Gestapo kill me. Let it be on their conscience. Should I not be able to bear the pain I would bash my head against the wall. And then I swore by Lenin to remain firm to my last breath, to the last drop of blood. The Gestapo would not get a single name out of me.

I was terrified when the cell door was opened next morning. But it was only the warder with a jug of water, and I was scared again when the lock turned at midday and in the evening. The Gestapo did not appear on that or on the following days but the uncertainty was most unnerving. One day the Gestapo came back, the stocky blond one with the green eyes – the most brutal of the thugs – with two others. This time they led me up the back stairs. Stopping at one of the landings, the one with the green eyes drew a gun from his breast pocket and ordered me to look through the window bars at the yard below. There at one of the corners was a patch sprinkled with sand with a broom beside it. 'On the way there you still have time to change your mind,' he said, waving the pistol in front of my eyes. My heart rose high up my throat, and then I suddenly felt firm and calm. They are going to shoot me, it was all over, and they had not got a single name from me.

They led me down to the cellar. There I was photographed and had my fingerprints taken. Then they walked with me past the house portal and through the cellar vault. And I longed at last to be at the corner of the wall. I went through a thousand terrors earlier but now I was resolute. However, they were only taking me to another interrogation.

Three further interrogation sessions followed. They would start with questions about my past, arrangements for meeting comrades, details of illegal work, descriptions of comrades. In the circumstances my memory was sharp and they could not catch me out. They hit me only with fists and boots, not the truncheon. What worried me greatly at this stage was their repeated threat that my obstinacy would expose my sister, whom they were also holding, to similar treatment.

The final interrogation went off peacefully. It was conducted by a single official. He even asked me to sit down and later offered me cigarettes and sweets, which I rejected. The written statement ran to some ten pages. It reiterated the same old story. I was being accused of being a leader of a group of Jewish Communist intellectuals. I don't know who was first to invent this story but it suited me well. Perhaps it was the Jewish names that I gave them, but it obviated linkage with the *Rotes Sprachrohr*. Nor did the Gestapo find out that Rudi Seidel was now the leader of the group.

During all the time at Alexanderplatz I was allowed exercise in the yard only once, when I met Rudi. We managed to walk one behind the other and agreed on what was to be said.

To complete the Liermann story: I saw him again in February 1937, when we were both witnesses at the trial of Rudi Seidel, I for the defence, and he for the prosecution. We were both left for a time in the witnesses' cell underneath the courtroom. He was afraid that I would attack him and said that when arrested the Gestapo already knew from another detainee about us, and that he had no choice but to confirm his story. This was most unlikely since I had no dealings with anyone of the district but himself, and no one but he knew the address of the Seidels' flat. After the liberation, in 1945, he became again a party functionary but several comrades, myself included, insisted that he be expelled from the party, and so he was.

On 9 May I was transferred to a prison in Moabit, one of the Berlin remand prisons. There, except for the last week, I was kept in solitary confinement for nine months. After four weeks I was allowed two books from the prison library: one on race theory and the other on National Socialism. The only other reading matter was the square pieces of lavatory paper cut from some newspaper bearing stock exchange news. These I studied but did not become an expert. At the end of six weeks I was permitted to subscribe to a newspaper. I chose the *Völkischer Beobachter*. This was the official organ of the Nazi Party but I was able to glean quite a lot of information from it.

We could also secretly exchange newspapers. A prisoner

across the corridor was getting another paper, the *Kurier* I think, and the convict-trusty of our block would push the papers under our doors. It is strange how stuck alone in a cell one acquires new senses. A word here and there on the so-called 'bear dance' (the daily exercise in the yard), and one discovers who one's neighbours are, politicals or criminals, who can be trusted and who can not. Sometimes one could send a written secret message [*Kassiber*] to a fellow prisoner, but this was dangerous; the convict-trusty of our block was a professional criminal.

On exercise I met a comrade I knew from the Youth League. He suggested that we offer some 'resistance': when ordered to run at the double during the 'bear dance' we were to drop out and stand aside. It was rather silly but I followed him. There is something emotionally satisfying in even useless disobedience.

My mother was allowed to visit me every three months. When she came first I wanted to embrace her but this was forbidden and the warder separated us. We had to sit across the table, and tears of joy at seeing me and also of worry ran down her cheeks. I tried to reassure her. I was her eldest son and also felt closest to her. I would spend the fifteen minutes of the visit in comforting her, explaining that unlike at Alexanderplatz nobody was maltreating me here – it all went routinely. On one of the visits the warder, who was a decent man, probably in the past a Social Democrat, peeped out to see that nobody was about and signalled with his hand that I could sit by my mother, embrace and kiss her. This, for a few minutes, was happiness.

Erich Mirek, a comrade from the *Rotes Sprachrohr* had been under arrest in 1933-34 in the notorious Columbia House [a former barracks which became the SS headquarters] and in Oranienburg concentration camp. He had been through a lot and seen many horrors. Nevertheless after his release he had the courage to send to me in prison the party dues which he collected from himself and two other comrades – 6 marks a month. I knew it was from him although he wrote my mother's name and address on the back of the envelope: the post-mark was from Wilmersdorf where he lived. It was a very dangerous thing to do for a man who was already under observation by the authorities. I used the money to pay for the newspaper and to buy a little extra food.

There were no further interrogations at Moabit. A lawyer came to see me once. He was sent to act in my defence. I had of course no money for a private advocate. He spoke to me briefly and rather sharply; he was probably a Nazi, perhaps even a Gestapo man, and we had little to say to each other.

My trial took place on 2 February 1937. I had received the Act of Indictment a fortnight earlier. In it I was accused, as expected, of being the leader of a Jewish Communist group. My mother was in the courtroom but the public had to leave when the trial started. When asked what I had to say in my defence I replied that I had nothing to say. The lawyer spoke and asked that the time on remand and in the police headquarters be taken into consideration. The public was then readmitted for the announcement of the verdict. I was given three and a half years for 'preparation of high treason' (a standard formula in those days) and was surprised that it was not more.[3] My mother broke down when she heard the sentence. When the trial ended the lawyer asked me what else he could do for me. I wanted him to reassure my mother, to tell her that I had already served a year of the sentence and that the rest would not be too hard for me. I hope that he did.

On 8 February I was taken from Moabit to the Brandenburg-Görden prison, and placed in a cell with a professional criminal.**"**

Notes

1. Rudi Arndt, born in 1909 in Berlin, joined the Young Communist League in 1928; earlier he had been active in Jewish organisations. As an official of the Young Communist League he was sentenced in 1931 to two and a half years' imprisonment. After release he became a member of the Young Communist League Central Committee. He was arrested again in 1933 and sentenced to three years of imprisonment, at the end of which he was taken in turn to Sachsenhausen, Dachau and Buchenwald where he became the *Älteste* of a Jewish hut. Standing up fearlessly for his fellow prisoners he earned the enmity of the SS. On 5 May 1940 he was driven through the guards' line and then shot. He died a few hours later.
2. Ernst Schneller, a teacher, was born 1890 in Leipzig. A member of the German Communist Party since 1920, he became a member of its Central Committee and was elected to the Reichstag in 1924. He was arrested by the Nazis in 1933 and sentenced to six years of prison at the end of which he

was sent to Sachsenhausen where he became one of the leaders of the clandestine resistance. He was murdered by the SS on 11 October 1944.

3. 'Preparation of high treason' was the legal basis, which had existed under the Weimar Republic, for condemning political opponents of the state. In general, defendants could be sentenced either to a term in an ordinary prison – *Gefängnis* – or the more rigorous *Zuchthaus*, which translates as 'penitentiary'. Under the Nazis all political convicts served their terms in a *Zuchthaus*. The generic English terms 'prison' and 'imprisonment' are, however, used throughout this book, as the individual records are not always specific, and the English usage does not distinguish between the two types of confinement.

4

Brandenburg-Görden Prison

"Brandenburg-Görden was a modern prison, built in 1929. Görden is an island in the River Havel and thus surrounded by a natural moat; it had two bridges across it which, if necessary, could be closed immediately. The corridors of the prison were divided at intervals by steel grilles. Two walls encircled the building, one five meters high, and guard dogs were kept in kennels by the walls. Experts regarded Brandenburg-Görden as one of the most secure gaols in Europe, and it was used during the Weimar Republic as a top security prison.

As I mentioned, I first shared a cell with a professional criminal. One of the problems with such prisoners was that they were entirely selfish. I always had the smallest piece of bread, the smallest herring, the most rotten potato. But in this respect my former life helped me to tolerate the situation.

By a stroke of luck I was later placed in a cell with two Communists. At that time cells for single prisoners were shared by two or even three prisoners. The oldest usually slept on a folding bunk, and the others on palliasses spread on the floor; at night no bare floor space was left. More than three-quarters of the inmates were anti-fascist political prisoners, mostly Communists. The work we had to do was to pluck sisal, a plant used for making cords to bind sheaves of corn at harvest time. We had to untangle the knots and straighten the stems of the plants. It was a dusty, dirty occupation, but this was compensated by the companionship of comrades. We spoke very softly so as not to be overheard outside the cell. Information was exchanged and discussed. News came haphazardly in all sorts of ways – on visiting the medical orderly, or through whispers whilst exercising in the yard.

My companions in that cell were Calel Lemer and Joseph Quatsch. I knew Calel already from the Communist Youth League before 1933; I could not have had a better companion. Quatsch was a functionary from one of our district centres. He had had considerable political experience, having been mainly engaged in work with Jewish comrades and organisations. We were allowed to receive letters and to write one every three months. Each letter received by my comrades was almost as good as having one of my own. We read our letters aloud to each other and got to know all our families intimately – we were indeed like brothers.

Later I was placed in a cell with two other anti-fascists, though one of them – Berger – was a Trotskyist. That was the beginning of a most valuable time for me. Rudolf Israelski was a doctor of philosophy and *Dozent* [Reader] at the Humboldt University; the other, Hans Berger, was a scientist and a specialist in physical chemistry. Since I had only primary school behind me, they undertook to extend my education. Teaching sessions were arranged. The prison had a library and the prisoner-librarian, Dr Glaser, was a friend of Israelski. We could order the required textbooks and Dr Glaser saw to it that these actually reached us. Two books could be exchanged by every prisoner each week. It was still the old library which had existed before 1933, because, for a time, the judicial authorities retained a certain independence, and the Nazis had probably overlooked the prison library when they held the book burnings.

I began to work systematically, specialising in physics, but also studying English and French. Israelski and Berger were serving very long sentences – fifteen and eight years respectively. They thought that my term of three and a half years was rather short to prepare for university entrance, but wanted me to take up physics after emigrating. My mother and friends were trying to obtain a permit for me to go to England, and actually succeeded in getting one.

The work we did in this cell was stripping feathers, and while engaged in it we gave and listened to lectures, on physics and other subjects. In the evenings we had to be on our palliasses at a fixed hour, I think it was 8 p.m. We had drawn chessboard squares on thick paper and made pieces from chewed-up bread. The black pieces were painted with shoe polish, the white left unstained. We would lie on our palliasses, heads close together, playing out our games, which sometimes lasted for days.

In the library, we found a book by Emile Coué, the philosopher and psychologist of autosuggestion. A patch of the sky could be seen through the bars of our cell window, and occasionally even a ray of sunlight broke in. We would stand breathing according to Coué's method, and repeated his maxim: 'Day by day, in every way I am getting better and better.' That is how we passed the time, the years, in our cell. Later, when in concentration camps, I looked back on this with a certain nostalgia.

Every day we had a so-called 'free hour' – actually, only half an hour, when we were marched single-file round a yard. Commands would be shouted — 'Halt!' 'Right!' 'Left!' — and the leading prisoner would demonstrate the usual physical jerks. We would also be ordered to sing, which we did with pleasure. We sang Heinrich Heine's 'Lorelei', but to a marching rhythm. What pleased us most was that it was a poem by a Jewish author, one who had also written:

Thinking of Germany in the night,
I lie awake and sleep takes flight …

Heine's books had of course been burned by the Nazis but no warder could associate the popular 'Lorelei' with him. We also sang other songs, particularly folk songs.

We were allowed to attend religious services and went each Saturday, within the prison, to a Jewish one, taken by a Rabbi from the town of Brandenburg. It may seem strange that a Rabbi was allowed to come and preach to us. No doubt it was another example of the relative independence of the prison authorities. We looked forward to it because there we met comrades from other parts of the large prison, could stand close to them and exchange news. A warder on duty stood behind the Rabbi while he was delivering his sermon and roared from time to time, 'Shut up, you bastards! Shut up, you swine!' The Rabbi would simply continue with the solemn, refined words of the sermon. At Passover Jews were given matzos [unleavened bread] to eat; the others had stolle [traditional German cake] at Christmas.

My mother visited me every three months until, as a Polish citizen, she was expelled from Germany in May 1938. She sold her few possessions and bought some bed linen with the proceeds so as not to arrive empty-handed at her paternal home; however all her goods were in any case confiscated at the frontier. My favourite uncle, who occasionally used to buy me a suit of clothes and invited me to his home for dinner every Sunday, came to see me once before leaving for the USA. He came after the *Kristallnacht* [9-10 November 1938, when Jews were attacked in reprisal for the assassination of a German diplomat by a young Polish Jew, and had their property destroyed all over Germany]. He knew about the concentration camps but, being a completely non-political person, thought it his moral duty to visit his nephew, a political convict, in prison. It was a very brave act and I have been grateful to him ever since.

My mother wrote several times to the director of the prison asking the authorities to reduce or remit my sentence. She begged the director to give me an opportunity to learn some useful trade, assuring him that I was a kind man who had never 'hurt a fly in his life', and that I was her sole support. Naturally, all this fell on deaf ears. It was some consolation that I was able to exchange letters with my sisters and brothers, who had all emigrated.

In the summer of 1938 I developed a feverish illness and was taken to the prison sick-bay. The orderlies there were prisoners. One of them took me to a proper bed with clean linen and brought me food. We did not know each other and so exchanged only a few words. Only later did I find out that it was Erich Honecker, the imprisoned leader of the Young Communist League. There was a resistance organisation in the prison but only a few people took a formal part in it, only those who met more or less regularly at, say, food distribution or work in the stores. I was one of the beneficiaries; a former Communist functionary of our

Prenzlauer Berg district, Hans Tübbecke, who had been the editor of the local illegal news sheet, *Der rote Stern* ('The Red Star'), began to bring me an extra piece of bread from time to time, which we shared between us in the cell. This help came by decision of the resistance group.

There was much to reward one for the wasted years in prison, primarily the wonderful comradeship of my cell-mates as we turned into a veritable band of brothers, and the progress in my education. All of us wore the same clothes and you learned to recognise the quality of people not by their exterior but by their character and reaction to common adversity. All this stood me in good stead later.

Anxiety began to mount as my release date drew nearer. Would I be released? The people whom I had invented at my interrogation to explain the provenance of the party dues I had collected were of course not found, and it was therefore likely that I would be turned over to the Gestapo, and that meant concentration camp. On the other hand, thanks to the efforts of my mother and a friend, who was already in England, I had a permit to go there after serving my sentence. Moreover, they would perhaps be inclined to expel me as a former Polish citizen.

I could hardly eat anything during the last few days in prison and left most of the food to my cell-mates. We were permitted to discuss personal welfare problems with the Rabbi. I explained to him that I had no home in Germany, no relatives and no friends. Where was I to go? He advised me to proceed to the Jewish Community Office in Berlin and ask for a place to stay. He would notify them about me.

Surprising as it might seem, I was actually released on 19 September 1939, nineteen days after the start of the war against Poland. However, now I was wary and feared a trick by the Gestapo. Would they follow me, see whom I met? I was seen off at the gate by the 'House Father', an official charged with the reception and discharge of prisoners and the custody of their documents and possessions. When we parted, he said not '*Aufwiedersehen*' [literally, 'till we meet again'] but '*Leben Sie Wohl*' [farewell]. There had been something odd about his attitude. My friend in England had provided me with new clothes to wear on release from prison, and the 'House Father' insisted that I wear this new suit and overcoat and not the old one. I feared that it would make me more easily recognisable to the Gestapo and therefore, once in the street, opened the suitcase and put on my old overcoat. I did not spot anyone following me.

The prison provided me with a ticket to Berlin and 3.50 marks. I went by tram to the railway station. In the compartment of the train was a man in a railwayman's uniform reading a newspaper with a worried look. Everyone else I saw looked worried, there certainly was no overt war enthusiasm. I saw people, particularly the older ones, who had been through the First World War, and evidently had a foreboding that the new one would not prove easy for them.

In Berlin I went, as instructed, to the Jewish Community Centre, and they found me a place for the night. I then went to the Palestine Office and explained to them that I had to register with the police within twenty-four hours and that as a former Polish citizen and now stateless, I would surely be interned, or worse. I had a permit to go to England. How could I get there? They advised me to go to the Dutch consulate nearby. There I found the waiting room full of Polish Jews, all looking for a way out of the country. I explained to an official that if I remained I would be sent to a concentration camp, and that I had a permit to enter England.

I also told him, perhaps misguidedly, that I had been a political prisoner. Anyhow, next morning I had a refusal from the Dutch. I returned to the Palestine Office. They were Zionists and knew that I was a Communist but nevertheless wanted to help me. But what could they do? They told me to register with the Hackischer Markt police station where they knew the officials to be relatively bland. I had no choice, nowhere to go, nowhere to hide – any attempt to contact comrades or friends could have greatly endangered them – and so I went. There I was told that as I had spent the previous night outside their area the station for me to register with was in the Kaiser Wilhelm Strasse. The official there looked at my papers, stood up and bawled out: 'A Jew, a Communist, a Pole! Sachsenhausen has long been yearning for such as you!'

I was locked up and taken that evening to the Grosse Hamburger Strasse, a collecting-point for Berlin Jews. The place is now marked by a plaque on a stone commemorating the deportation of 50,000 people to concentration camps where almost all perished. And that was also my point of departure for Sachsenhausen.**99**

5

Sachsenhausen

The Nazis began to intern people as soon as they seized power, but later built specially designed concentration camps. Sachsenhausen, built in 1936, was the second oldest of these; Dachau, near Munich, was the first. Ravensbrück, to the north of Sachsenhausen – a camp for women – and Buchenwald, near Weimar, followed. The main camps sprouted temporary or permanent satellite ones, so that the whole of Germany was soon heavily studded with concentration camps. Other camps were built in the occupied countries. In time the network included fifteen main and 500 auxiliary camps; these were manned by 40,000 SS men. By a conservative count 1,600,000 prisoners passed through the camps and of these 1,180,650 perished. This is not counting those killed immediately on arrival; the sum total of all victims, including those in the so-called extermination camps, amounts to about 11,000,000.

Sachsenhausen lies some thirty kilometres to the north of Berlin near the town of Oranienburg, which had its own earlier and speedily improvised concentration camp in a local brewery. When Hüttner was brought to Sachsenhausen it held 12,000 prisoners in fifty huts, two and later three of which were used for Jews. These three huts, with a group of other huts to the right of the main entrance, formed a so-called 'small camp', separate from the 'main' camp, and the Jewish prisoners there lived under an even more cruel regime. Twenty-eight other huts were used for services, such as stores, offices, disinfection and quarantine, workshops and the sick-bay (*Krankenbau*). Six were reserved for prisoners of war, but they were often killed on arrival. Each hut was designed for 146 prisoners but at times held as many as 400 or 500 who slept at first on the floor and later in three- or four-tiered bunks, frequently two or even three sharing a palliasse on the same bunk. A special hut, or bunker, formed the camp prison, containing eighty small cage-like cells. Here the prisoners were exposed to especially brutal and sadistic treatment. Thus, for example, two English prisoners were held there in complete darkness chained to a concrete block prior to their execution. Among the prisoners elsewhere in the camp were Pastor Martin Niemöller and the French statesmen, Georges Mandel, Paul Reynaud and Yves Delbos.

Station Z, ominously designated by the last letter of the alphabet, began to be built in 1940. It was a complex of buildings designed for the murder of prisoners who were not to be executed in the presence of the whole camp population at the evening roll-call on the barrack square. It was in this Z station that 18,000 Soviet prisoners of war were killed, 15,000 of them at a mock medical inspection, when they stood next to SS men masquerading as medical orderlies. They had their backs against a height-measuring board and were then shot in the nape of the neck through a slit in the wall behind them. Station Z also contained a gas chamber, a crematorium with four ovens, and gallows for the simultaneous hanging of four victims. Portable equipment stores included another gallows, a trolley for flogging and a special pole for the public hanging of prisoners by the wrists tied at their back (*Pfahlhängen*), so that, when raised, the prisoner's shoulders were dislocated and the surrounding ligaments torn.

Most huts stood concentrically in three or four semi-circles around a semi-circular barrack square located directly behind the main entrance, with its wrought iron gate, which bore the derisive inscription '*Arbeit macht frei*' (Work makes one free).

The camp was surrounded by a 2.7 metre high stone wall with on its inside an electrified (1,000 watt) barbed wire fence. So-called *Spanishe Ritter* (Spanish riders) – barbed wire wound round wooden stands – stood in front of the electrified fence. Nine watchtowers equipped with search-lights were manned day and night by SS guards armed with rifles and machine guns. Escape was well nigh impossible although a few prisoners managed to flee while working in one of the squads on detail outside the camp and in 1944 two escaped from the camp itself. Outside the camp walls were stone buildings for the SS, their *Kommandatur* (headquarters), villas and other buildings for the higher officers and their families. These were surrounded by another fence and watchtowers.

A few huts at the edge of the camp formed a separate unit. Barbed wire covered them from ground to roof, the windows were opaque, and guards were on permanent duty inside. The prisoners in them, numbering up to 150, were brought from various concentration camps; all were Jewish and specialists in one or other of the graphic arts. They were employed on a project innocuously called *Aktion Bernhard*, and none was to remain alive after the completion of his task – the manufacture of fake English and American banknotes and counterfeit personal documents for Nazi agents in neutral and enemy countries.

It is claimed that in spite of every precaution a few prisoners, including Kurt Lewinsky and Leo Krebs, secreted a couple of the banknotes and smuggled these out one night to a comrade in the main camp – the well-known Communist leader Robert Uhrig, who undertook to pass the information on along his channels. Whether he succeeded or not, a few weeks later the RAF dropped a couple of incendiary bombs on the hut. These did little damage but Lewinsky hoped that it was a sign that the message had reached proper quarters. In February 1945, when the Soviet Army began to approach, the equipment and personnel were moved away to Mauthausen, a camp near Linz, in Austria. It was planned to continue *Aktion Bernhard* there, but the American army soon overran the area and the prisoners were rescued.

Probably on account of its proximity to Berlin, Sachsenhausen was used by Himmler as a command centre for the whole of the concentration camp system, as well as for the training of guards and officers. One of the latter was the notorious future commandant of Auschwitz – Höss.

In the earlier camps some lip-service was paid by the Nazis to the 're-education' of prisoners, but the guiding principle underlying the planning of all the later concentration camps and the regime therein was, subject to special local needs and appropriate modification, similar throughout: the aim was to exterminate most of the prisoners by starvation and work. Those judged unfit were murdered at once. Mortality among the prisoners was always high. Of 200,000 brought to the camp between 1939 and 1945 at least 100,000 perished. The SS's chief doctor in the camp, Baumkötter, testified before a Soviet military court that 8,000 prisoners died there from starvation between August 1942 and April 1945 and that a further 26,000 dystrophic men deemed unfit for work were sent away for extermination elsewhere. (The term dystrophy is used for the last stage of starvation, when irreversible metabolic changes set in the organism. Such a prisoner was sometimes referred to as a *Muselmann*.)

Working squads (*Kommandos*) were formed for work inside the camp, and also outside in plants owned by the SS or various industrial firms. A particularly feared detail was the *Klinkerwerk* (brick works) where the ground had to be levelled for the construction of the plant extensions. Here the prisoners were often ordered to work at the double and many died every day.

Medical aid was always inadequate. Prisoners reporting sick were cursed and shouted at. Jews were at first denied all medical help at the sick-bay and help had to be organised surreptitiously by the resistance organisation. At times medical experiments were performed on prisoners, e.g. gangrenous wounds were produced to test the effect of new drugs. Poisoned bullets and hand grenades were tried out, particularly on Russian prisoners of war. Attempts to induce infectious hepatitis were undertaken in children aged between eight and fourteen. Epidemics occurred of meningitis, typhoid and typhus fever, entailing heavy mortality.

Prisoners guilty of minor offences were placed in a special penal company and subjected to particularly severe treatment. One was the testing of army boots. Factories were constantly manufacturing new types of boots and these were tried out by prisoners of the penal company. A special track was laid around the barrack-square with a surface reproducing different kinds of ground over which soldiers would have to march, such as a ploughed field, metalled road, marsh, swamp, sandy beach and river bottom. Prisoners were made to wear these specimen boots, which were often too tight or too large for them, and march around the square for a distance of forty kilometres every day, often at the double, and carrying a pack containing fifteen kilos of sand.

A constantly recurring physical and mental trauma was the roll-call on the barrack square conducted at first three times and later twice a day. Work-squads would be formed in the morning. In the evening they would return bearing with them those who died or were killed during the day. All would be made to watch public executions, floggings, hanging and hanging by the wrists. It is recorded that between March 1941 and November 1942 there were 1,000 public floggings and 600 hangings by the wrists. A frequent general punishment for all prisoners was prolonged standing on the barrack square for hours on end, in rain, heat or frost, in their threadbare clothes. Food and water were withheld. This punishment was inflicted when a prisoner was unaccounted for at roll-call; he could have died, for example, somewhere outside the camp and not have been brought back by his comrades. It is recorded that on 19 January 1940 prisoners stood for sixteen hours and 430 of them froze to death. Sometimes, to amuse themselves, the SS would order prisoners to do exercises – press-ups, knee-bends, and rolling in the mud and snow, all to the jeers and kicks of the guards.

The conditions in the camp, always grim, grew steadily worse as war progressed and the Allied forces continued their relentless advance. Nevertheless, in spite of the terror, organised resistance did not cease. As we shall see many of the prisoners survived due in large measure to the help they received from members of the resistance. If not themselves members of the resistance the beneficiaries were, for reasons of security, left unaware of the origin of the help. Most of the resistance leaders were experienced and determined men, mostly Communists, such as Ernst Schneller, but some Social Democrats, Christians and others were also involved. Certain principles were invariably observed. The stronger helped the weaker. Equality in the distribution of food, clothing, fuel and 'privileges' was strictly enforced. Special importance was attached to assistance for inexperienced new arrivals and Jews and, after the outbreak of the war, to foreigners, such as Czechs and Russians. Morale was maintained by dissemination of news, cultural work, personal contacts and the observance of special occasions such as birthdays and working-class holidays.

In all camps certain administrative functions were entrusted to prisoners chosen by the SS. These were so-called *Ältestes* – camp *Älteste*, hut *Älteste*, bay *Älteste*, sick-bay *Älteste*. (There is no fully satisfactory English term for the German *Älteste*, literally 'oldest', as used in this context. Some authors have translated it as 'senior' but this hardly conveys the considerable power and authority wielded by this functionary.) Another prisoner functionary was the head of a work squad – a *Kapo*. Desirable posts of influence were also in offices, kitchen, stores and the sick bay. The resistance organisation tried to have as many of these positions as possible filled by reliable comrades. This was at times achievable because professional criminals, whom the SS would have preferred, were not only brutal but also dishonest and inefficient.

Despite strict measures of conspiratorial security, resistance cost many lives. In Sachsenhausen a particularly heavy blow fell on 11 October 1944 when 27 leaders, including Ernst Schneller and three French comrades, were betrayed by an informer and executed.

The camp was liberated by the Soviet army in April 1945 but a few days earlier 33,000 prisoners had been forced out to march north, apparently to be loaded into lighters and drowned in the Baltic. 6,000 died on the way from exhaustion, starvation or the bullets of the escort. The rest were freed by the advancing columns of the Soviet army. Only 3,000 were left in the camp, mostly women, children and some of the sick.

Sachsenhausen is now a memorial of 'Remembrance and Warning' (*Mahn- und Gedenkstätte*). Most of the huts have been demolished but a few are left as exhibits, as are some of the watchtowers and the main entrance. The walls have been razed to the ground. A few impressive monuments have been erected. There is a museum displaying mementoes of the camp and portraits of some of the resistance leaders. A cinema shows a film of the camp as found on liberation.

Similar memorials, some smaller but at least one – at Buchenwald – even larger, are scattered through the German Democratic Republic. A few memorials are also maintained in other countries: Poland, Czechoslovakia, and the Federal German Republic. In the German Democratic Republic they are visited by thousands of people, schoolchildren, students, delegations of factory workers, German and Soviet soldiers. Children in the GDR are encouraged to go through a secular confirmation ceremony at the age of fourteen, a step in becoming a fully fledged citizen, and most do so. In preparation for it they are taken to one of the camp memorials and see for themselves something of the satanic state that their republic has replaced.

6

Jonny Hüttner in Sachsenhausen

66On that September day in 1939, at the collecting point for Berlin Jews, we were stuffed into two cages of a closed police van with bars over the windows and the skylight and alighted at the end of the journey to shouts of 'At the double!' and a shower of blows. It was raining, and our first sight of the camp was its barrack square with about 100 prisoners rolling on the ground and the SS standing over them kicking the slower ones with their boots. Running, we reached the disinfection huts where we had to take off all our clothes and step under the cold showers. Nobody explained what to do, mistakes were unavoidable, and each one led to blows by the SS: beating newcomers gave them special pleasure. I was one of those beaten under the shower. Prison clothes were thrown over to us. We had to put them on whether they fitted or not, but shoes we could more or less exchange between ourselves. Then we had to run and line up in front of Hut 39, where with a few short interruptions I was to remain for the next three years (that particular hut still stands as an exhibit in the Sachsenhausen Memorial). While waiting in front of it I saw the anguished face of a youngish man inside the hut straining to keep himself up to the window, licking the moisture off the glass.

We entered the dormitory which measured eight metres by twelve and then held 300 prisoners. We had to sleep on the floor (three-tiered bunks were installed later). The floor space available to each prisoner was only one-third of a metre and we had to sleep two or three on one palliasse, on our sides, back to front. After leaving one's space at night to

Hut 39 in Sachsenhausen in which Jonny Hüttner lived from September 1939 to October 1942

relieve oneself there was nowhere to return. Later we arranged a nightly roster for one of us to stay awake and guard the space for the returning prisoners. The windows were nailed down and strips of paper pasted over their margins to render them completely airtight, and so was the roof ventilator shaft. The foreboding that the hut had been prepared for the gassing of all of us sprang to mind. A few of us were political prisoners brought here after serving prison sentences. All were Jews – and most were Polish or former Polish citizens. Were we all now hostages to be killed should the Polish campaign, now in its third week, run into unforeseen trouble?

Nights in the airtight dormitory were terrible, but the days were worse. Each hut had two dormitories and in the mornings all were forced into one of these and made to lie down prone on the floor. Every two or three hours the SS would enter and order press-ups, up and down on command, until we were utterly exhausted. The older men could hardly do one press-up, and the SS beat them with sadistic pleasure. This torture would go on for about fifteen minutes and then they would proceed to the next hut. Dense steam, as in a laundry, would fill the dormitory; we had nothing to drink, and that is why the man I saw on arrival tried so desperately to lick condensed moisture off the glass panes. About twenty prisoners died each day as the result of this procedure. That there were not more we owed to our hut *Älteste*, the Cologne Communist Jupp Adorf, who had been a prisoner since 1933. He did what he could to help us; as soon as the SS left he would bring in bowls of drinking water and let in some air by keeping the door open. After some time the SS realised that there were fewer deaths in our hut than elsewhere. They dismissed Adorf and put him on half rations. Then it was our turn to help him: a fellow prisoner, Leo Hauser, and myself saved a slice of bread out of our daily ration and placed it in a prearranged spot where Adorf would pick it up in the mornings.

On 27 September 1939 the door of the hut flew open for the Camp Commandant with a few other SS officers. Solemnly he announced: 'The Polish campaign has ended with our complete victory. Open the windows!' Workmen with their tools appeared, drew out the nails, threw open the windows and freed the ventilator shaft. We now had more air but, alas, no other amelioration. Actually, at night the windows and the door had to be kept closed and there was still a lack of air. Each hut had a dormitory at either end, and in the centre a latrine, a washroom, a closet for cleaning utensils and a living space with tables and benches. Trying to relieve the unbearable overcrowding in the dormitories Adorf moved the young prisoners at night to the living space. This gave them a little more room and air.

One night the SS entered looking for fun and ordered 'Jews up!' Thick dust rose from under the palliasses and filled the air. The mass of prisoners rushed to the door where the SS stood and hit out at everyone with spade handles. Further blows drove us round the hut. Some prisoners fell, never to rise again. Then they ordered us to squat and we had to stay squatting, barefoot and in our shirts. It was January and the temperature was −20° centigrade. Our good hut *Älteste* was no longer with us and there was no one to help us. Limbs were frozen, the affected men could not stand upright at roll-call next morning and were again severely beaten. 100 died following that night. At that time Jews were denied medical help and many developed pneumonia, abscesses and gangrene. Some of the medical orderlies, among them the Breslau Communist Walter Blass, repeatedly risked their lives by secretly bringing us dressings, drugs and other medical supplies.

The SS were forever inventing new ways of taunting and tormenting us. One day they called 'Fathers and sons, forward!' and commanded them to punch each other's face in turn. When the sons refused, they showed them 'how it should be done'. Another time they called for a Rabbi, dragged him to the latrine 'to hold a Jewish service for the SS', and we heard his anguished cries as they beat him to death.

Although so many were dying, overcrowding never eased because new contingents kept arriving. They came from all parts of Germany, after the Polish campaign mostly from Poland, and thereafter from all parts of occupied Europe. Thus between 300 and 400 men always remained in the hut.

Behind our hut stood another for non-Jewish Polish boys aged between fourteen and seventeen. They had held a celebration of one of their national holidays in their school yard. The Nazis got wind of it, arrested the lot and brought them to Sachsenhausen.

The resistance group in the main camp succeeded in getting a very decent man, Franz Bobzien, appointed as the boys' *Älteste*. This was quite an achievement for it could well have been a professional criminal. But the boys hated all Germans and it was difficult for Franz to gain their confidence. Years later, after the liberation, I met one of the boys again, now a journalist, and he told me about the inner conflict that they had experienced: they hated Franz, who later perished in the camp, as a German but were gradually won over by his kindness and sympathy. In the end they came to understand that there were Germans and Germans. Franz Bobzien was a Social Democrat but he co-operated with Communists and it was thanks to the resistance organisation, headed by Ernst Schneller, that he was made hut *Älteste*.

Early in 1940 I broke the fibula of my left leg. At the time there was no treatment for Jews in the sick-bay, hence the comrades of the main camp organised the treatment for me. Franz Cyranek removed the Jewish star from my tunic and then presented me to the SS doctor, Orthmann, whom I was to meet again in my last concentration camp. Since I wore no star on my chest he could and did order an X-ray, whereupon I was admitted to hospital and had a plaster of Paris bandage applied. I remained an in-patient and the comrades saw to it that I had an extra piece of bread each day since I was in a poor state of health. I was kept for six weeks in hospital because the comrades knew that I would be helpless outside.

Only a few of us were made to work during our first months at Sachsenhausen, and that occasionally – clearing snow along the camp wall to give the guards a clearer path and view. The rest of us remained in the huts but had to stand there lined up all day long. In late January 1940, we were allocated to proper work squads [*Kommandos*].

First I was put into the *Klinkerwerk* squad. A brick factory was being enlarged, and we had to level and deepen the ground for the foundations of the buildings. We worked with spades and pickaxes lifting heavy clay soil and stones, and loading up wagonettes. A shrill whistle would signal the approach of the engine that was to pull away the wagonettes, and woe betide the prisoner whose wagonette was not filled to the brim. Then I worked for a time as a joiner and learned to deal with wood and timber. And I also worked in some of the so-called Speer[1] work-squads as an electrician installing electric light in newly built huts and workshops.

Digging with spade and pickaxe was always troublesome; you had an SS man somewhere by your side constantly shouting, 'Move on! Get on! Hurry, hurry!' Electrical work was much more comfortable. One stood on a ladder and drilled holes for sockets and cables in concrete and wood. For a time I was on so-called hut duties. I had to clean and tidy everything, stow away the palliasses in the morning and lay them out in the approved manner. Everything had to be ship-shape for the SS inspection. While on this work I developed inflammation of one of my eyes. It had to be covered up and I could only use the other one. As well as cleaning I drew birthday-cards for comrades. What with a single eye, the pictures were not too good, and so I wrote all sorts of poems to go with them. Well, perhaps not real poems, only doggerel verse, but the recipients were well enough pleased with them. For a time I was also a glazier, also in one of the Speer work squads.

A very dangerous time began for me in May 1942, when I was sent with a work squad to Drögen, a village near the town of Fürstenberg, some ninety kilometres north of Berlin. The place had been previously used as a police training school; now it was a training centre for agents and execution squads for the occupied territories. Most instructors and service personnel were German SS, the 'students' were foreigners – Croats, Ukrainians and Latvians. We heard that they had been recruited among criminals in the jails of their countries, not that there were not also fascist-minded thugs among them recruited elsewhere – those not averse to murder for pay. We were to build a sports ground for them, and that meant levelling the ground, as in the Sachsenhausen *Klinkerwerk*.

Each prisoner had to load three cubic metres of earth an hour into wagonettes. This proved very hard; my hands swelled up and I developed tenosynovitis [a painful inflammation of the tendons of the hands and fingers]. My mate was a professional criminal who expected me to do part of his work. When I refused he hit me with his spade across my back and this made things even more difficult. Relief came from the local resistance group.

When we were being drafted for dispatch to Drögen I was given a *Kassiber* (a secret written message) to one of the leaders of the resistance there, the late Eduard Besch.[2] This served as my introduction and proved in the end to be my salvation.

At roll call one morning, knowing that electricians were needed, he mentioned to the SS officer that he had found one, a good craftsman, but a Jew. Besch, of course, was no anti-Semite but had to speak in this way. And so two of us, both prisoners, the other a trained electrician, began laying electric light in the new barracks.

One day the head of the training school, a high-ranking SS officer, saw me at work in his study. On the walls of his room hung pictures of human heads and skulls with corresponding measurements. They were for teaching race 'sciences'. The officer, as if thinking aloud, said that in the East all Jews were being liquidated. My hands dropped: I recalled that my last letter to my mother was returned marked 'Deported' in blue pencil. I knew now that she had been murdered.

In Sachsenhausen we were allowed to sing on Sunday mornings, and a few weeks later I wanted to start doing so in Drögen, where the practice was hitherto unknown. I taught my fellow prisoners one of our songs. This must have been reported to the SS. Next day at work the NCO in charge, Hauptscharführer Bogdalle, well known for his brutality, began beating me, and that evening at roll call the camp *Älteste* heard him say, 'That Jew won't last another eight days here.'

I was taken off electrical work and returned to pick and shovel. In the mornings, at dinner time and in the evenings I had to squat and in that posture hop frogwise on command. I also had to roll on the ground with Bogdalle kicking me with his boots. My food ration was cut; I was issued only one instead of two pieces of bread daily and only a half portion of soup. However, on returning to the hut, and it was an SS hut with lockers in it, I would find a large piece of bread in my locker. Where it came from I did not know; it was not safe to know. Later I discovered that it was brought by Eduard Besch. Luckily, on the fifth day Bogdalle was posted away and the new NCO knew nothing of the affair. (After the war Bogdalle was employed by a Munich hotel. He was recognised by some former prisoners, arrested and sentenced in West Germany to threefold life imprisonment. Released after fifteen years he later retired to an old peoples' home.)

Electricians were still wanted and Besch found another job for me, this time outside the camp in a private house in the town of Fürstenberg. I would set out from the camp in the morning with my tools, escorted by an SS guard. My task was to extend the electricity to the second floor of the house, actually the attic. The house belonged to a cigarette manufacturer. His main residence was in Berlin but he had come here to escape the bombing. The SS, however, had requisitioned the house and moved him to the attic. Prisoners were forbidden to speak to civilians and I did not reply to his questions. His wife looked at me also with a certain sympathy, and as she passed would quickly put down a piece of bread while her husband would likewise somewhere 'forget' a handful of cigarettes. I did not smoke myself but took the bread and cigarettes back to the camp for those who needed them. I ate the food left over for me by the guard; it was good SS food and there was enough of it.

When the Fürstenberg job ended I was given another in the SS kitchen. Here I worked with imprisoned Czech students and Dutch army officers. They would supply me with a whole loaf of bread from the SS stores and this I shared with comrades in our barracks.

One day all Jews were told not to report for work. Besch found out that we were being sent back to Sachsenhausen. This was ominous since there was still work to be done and we were needed in Drögen. In May of that year, following the action of the Jewish Communist Herbert Baum resistance group which distributed anti-Nazi leaflets, painted slogans and finally set fire to an exhibition organised under the title of 'The Soviet Paradise' in the Berlin Lustgarten (now Marx Engels Square), the SS retaliated by shooting 100 of our prisoners in the Sachsenhausen Z station. Then they brought another 250 from Berlin and shot them in the same place. All went to their death unresisting. So, when a lorry came to collect us we feared that it might be our last journey. As we made for the lorry at the double, Besch parted from us with the words 'One dies easier when fighting. You feel no pain when fighting!' Some of us decided there and then that we would not submit without resistance as the earlier victims had done in May.

That night, back in Sachsenhausen, I related to the comrades all I had heard about the fate of Jews in the East and about the execution squads which were being trained in Drögen, and we all agreed that when our turn came we would not go without a fight. Twelve days later, on 22 October 1942, we were stopped from mustering for work and were locked up in the huts. I shall return to the events of that day after speaking first about some of my fellow prisoners.

Most Jewish prisoners were of course non-political. They were petty traders and artisans – tailors, shoemakers, carpenters, plumbers. Many had been living in Berlin and had been rounded up in the course of the early campaign against Polish Jews. German Jews came later. One was a man called Müller, a much decorated First World War air ace. Politically he was of the right, a member of the German National Party, of which he spoke openly. Having had to obtain some personal papers it had been found that he had some Jewish ancestors. Initially in camp he wanted to have nothing to do with the 'Jewish lot', and showed a distinct aversion to Polish Jews. But he had to wear the Jewish star and was beaten just like the rest of us. To the SS it did not matter whether you were an eighth, a quarter or a full Jew; you wore the star and were treated accordingly. Müller thought that he would be helped from outside but no help came. Step by step he began to submit to the common fate. He sensed that organised resistance functioned in the camp and tried to come closer to it.

Müller had been unlucky. The definition of Jewishness was

sometimes arbitrary. My comrade, Werner Rosenberg, joined the Communist Party in 1932 and was arrested for the first time in 1933. They beat him severely but fortunately sent him to a hospital. There, after recovery, they simply discharged him. He lived illegally and for a few years did various underground jobs, the last one as a 'technician', in other words printing a newspaper with his brother, called *Die Wahrheit*. They arrested him again in 1936 and in December of that year sentenced him to three years imprisonment. We first met in Brandenburg–Görden. On release they took him back for seven weeks to the police headquarters at Alexanderplatz at the end of which the Gestapo man said, 'Herr Rosenberg, you are going to a retraining camp for a few months.' Well, it turned out to be six years and there was little retraining.

In Sachsenhausen he was initially placed in the main camp as a *Reichsdeutsche* (non-Jew)[3] but then they called him to the office and said, 'You are a Jew.' He replied, 'My father is half Jewish, and my mother is non-Jewish.' The SS man responded, 'No, you are a Jew and are going to the small camp.' In Hut 39 we were together and together we were sent to Auschwitz–Monowitz. There, after a while he became non-Jewish again, worked in the kitchen and was even made a *Kapo*. Blass, who was working in the office, told him that a letter had arrived there ordering a reclassification as Jews of people like him, who had earlier been classified as non-Jews. The SS chief clerk, a stupid man who often relied on Blass's advice, asked him what he was to do, and Blass told him to do nothing. Later, another letter came asking for a report on action taken on the previous order, and the chief clerk consulted Blass again. Blass said, 'There is even less reason for action now. The Russians will soon be here.' So Rosenberg remained a *Reichsdeutsche*. His brother had been taken to Sachsenhausen three months after him. He was never classified as a Jew, worked in the pharmacy and was often able to smuggle medical supplies to us, thus saving many lives. Some prisoners knew that he had a Jewish brother in the camp but the SS never found this out.

Some time later the chief pharmacist in Sachsenhausen asked Rosenberg's brother if it was true that he had a brother in Auschwitz and if so wouldn't he like to be together with him. His brother replied, 'Yes, if it were possible.' The Sachsenhausen pharmacy supplied some drugs to Auschwitz and the next time the chief pharmacist visited Auschwitz on duty he searched Rosenberg out in the kitchen. All he asked was, 'Are you Rosenberg?' and left, but an order arrived subsequently to transfer him to Sachsenhausen, and he worked there with his brother in the pharmacy until they were liberated by the Soviet Army on 22 April 1945.

I recall another prisoner called Fränkel, who was an expert on art and owner of a firm dealing with interior decoration, paintings and sculptures. He had designed and supplied objects of art and decoration for various mansions and palaces, including the Reich President's, and had arranged the interior decoration of the Reich Chancellery. He was an excellent lecturer, and when we were forced to stand all day in the dormitory, Fränkel would deliver fascinating talks on art and art history. It ended badly for him. One day the SS collected prisoners with some deformity or defect, such as hernia, cataract, a missing limb and so on. There were about 100 of them and they were taken away in small groups, among them Fränkel, although he was perfectly fit. A few hours later artificial limbs, hernia trusses, dentures and spectacles were returned and we knew that all the prisoners had been killed. We discovered later that the killing was by suffocation with vehicle exhaust-fumes.

Another interesting lecturer was the Austrian Viktor Stein, an expert on the buildings, churches and monuments of his native Vienna. At one time we had to stand not in the dormitory but in the washroom and it was there that Stein talked enthusiastically on the beauty of his beloved city.

Among prisoners a few were relatively 'privileged'. They had softer jobs, working as batmen to the SS or as servants in their canteen and office. They were exempted from roll-calls, wore cleaner clothes, were better nourished and some gave themselves airs. They were of course disliked. We called them *die Prominenten* [the elite] and often poked fun at them.

After the isolation of the Jewish huts ended and we were placed in various work squads, we mustered for the roll-call with all the others on the main barrack square; we were also able to walk and talk to other prisoners on Sunday afternoons. Among the latter were Polish academics from Cracow University. They had been invited one day to a conference in their university assembly hall and, when seated, an SS officer had announced: 'Gentlemen, henceforth we shall remain together.' They were loaded on to lorries just as they were, in their academic robes with regalia, then taken by freight trains to Sachsenhausen to be received there with customary SS hospitality.

From the time of my study of physics at Brandenburg I was intrigued by the so-called Doppler principle, particularly how it could be reconciled with the relativity theory. I wanted to discuss this with a Polish physicist. Our former hut *Älteste*, Adorf, pointed one out to me. I approached him one Sunday afternoon and asked permission to discuss the problem with him. We walked around the square and talked. He thought that the Doppler principle could be reconciled with the relativity theory by means of the Lorentz transformation, and explained how to do it.[4]

Two comrades in Sachsenhausen became my closest friends – Calel Lemer and Leo Hauser, and I want to say something about each one of them.

Calel Lemer, born in 1913, joined the Young Communist League and was a most intelligent, tireless and enthusiastic party activist. He lived in our district of Berlin and we became friends. An electrician by trade, he was, like most of us, often unemployed. In 1934 my mother was unable to pay the rent and we were evicted. We stood in the yard with our furniture: mother and three children, the two younger ones crying loudly. Opposite lived a worker, a Social Democrat. He opened the window and spoke loudly and fiercely about the inhumanity of throwing a mother and children into the street when so many flats stood empty. Other windows opened, tenants listened and kept quiet. Calel took me into his room. He had only a single bed but we both shared it until my mother found other accommodation.

Like me, Calel was arrested and sentenced to three and a half years. We were together in Brandenburg-Görden, then in Sachsenhausen and were also transferred in October 1942 jointly to Auschwitz-Monowitz where he took part in our

Calel Lemer in 1934

resistance group's most daring undertakings. He very nearly lost his life when a group of three comrades planning an escape needed a pair of insulated pliers with which to cut the electrified barbed wire of the fence. Calel was an electrician and got them one. The comrades were betrayed by their Polish contact. They were arrested and thrown into the bunker. The source of the pliers could not remain secret and Calel was also accused with the group. However, despite torture the leader of the group succeeded in convincing the SS that Calel knew nothing of the escape plan; he merely lent them the pliers. They were hanged; Calel was saved.

When Auschwitz was evacuated we were transferred together to Dora concentration camp, of which I shall speak later. When the Americans came close to it, the SS called for all Ukrainians, Russians and Jews to step forward. Calel had been warned not to do so and to hide, but he was proud and decided to share the fate of the others. They were formed into a column and driven into a barn which was then firmly closed. Those few who broke out were mowed down by SS machine guns. Next day the SS set it alight and all the prisoners perished in the flames. Only charred bodies were found by the Americans. Calel Lemer has no grave, no plaque, no record. These recollections are his only memorial.

My second friend, Leo Hauser, has fortunately outlived the Third Reich. On arrival in Sachsenhausen I began to look for someone of my way of thinking. Leo attracted my attention by his modest bearing and courtesy to fellow prisoners. He was not, like some, constantly comparing his portion of soup with that of others. In conversation he was thoughtful, even-tempered and considerate. Very soon we decided to share the same palliasse. Later, when a Communist Party group was formed, Leo was with us although not himself a member of the party. He had our unqualified trust. At the time it was not a question of confronting the Nazis – only of mutual aid – and Leo was useful in rejecting certain sectarian attitudes on our part. For example, some prisoners liked to collect cigarette-ends and exchange these for bread; a few of our comrades loathed this habit and showed hostility to the tobacco collectors. Leo remained generous. All prisoners who behaved decently to each other were comrades as far as he was concerned, and so we gradually built a feeling of real community in our hut without classifying prisoners into party and non-party. I also tended to be sectarian – towards Trotskyists, for example – but began gradually to realise that one could work with anyone so long as the leadership remained in trustworthy hands.

Leo was one of a large Polish Jewish family of eight children. A trained furrier, he had worked for some of the Berlin ready-to-wear stores. In 1934 he took his only daughter to one of his sisters in Paris, and heard no more about them while in the concentration camp. His wife died from natural causes in 1940; he received a last letter from her, which was a terrible blow for him. After liberation he discovered that his sister had taken his daughter to Switzerland where she was brought up as a Christian in a Protestant pastor's family.

In October 1942 Leo was transferred with myself and others to Auschwitz-Monowitz where he worked at first as a medical orderly and then with a 'flak' work-squad, building concrete foundations for anti-aircraft guns. As in Sachsenhausen he enjoyed the full confidence of the resistance group. In fact, he was a tower of strength, being brave and intelligent and yet cautious – turning down, for example, wild escape plans.

On 18 January 1945, during the evacuation of the camp, he was one of the five prisoners who managed to escape with the resistance leader, Leon Stasiak. They were joined in flight by another five escaping separately; all ten were hidden until the arrival of the Soviet army. He returned to Berlin in 1946. Leo always wanted to become a doctor and this eventually proved possible. Early in his studies he met a fellow student, Hannelore, whom he married. He had always lived in West Berlin and remained there after qualifying as a doctor, working in East Berlin hospitals – and became thus, after the division of Berlin, one of the few commuters who travelled from west to east every day. He joined the Socialist Unity Party and was a loyal, though not an uncritical member. Although it was a difficult decision, he established contact with his daughter in Switzerland and the rest of his family in

Paris and Israel. On a visit to Israel, in 1981, he had a heart attack whilst swimming in the sea and died.

I must now say something about our resistance work in Sachsenhausen. By the beginning of 1940 we had a group of ten or twelve comrades who had had experience of political work before Hitler and then of prison and concentration camps. Most were Communists, a few were Social Democrats, while Leo Hauser was not a member of any party. The leader of our group was the already mentioned Breslau Communist, Walter Blass. Among the rest were Horst Jonas, Gottfried Ballin and Erich Markowitsch, all of whom later played a prominent part in the public life of the German Democratic Republic.

The earliest and most pressing need in the camp was for mutual aid. We tried to help as many as possible of our fellow prisoners to survive, and to do that it was essential to ensure a just distribution of food and clothes with an extra supply for the weak and sick. Likewise it could sometimes be arranged for the weak to be given lighter work. All such initiatives had to be set in train by our comrades in the main (non-Jewish) camp who had a powerful resistance organisation with some of their members in key positions, such as clerks in offices, medical orderlies and workers in stores. Their clandestine organisation was efficient. They were, of course, more numerous than we in the small camp and being non-Jewish were less exposed to SS persecution. They could at times help with supplies and even conceal some particularly vulnerable comrades.

The next task was political work among the young. We had about 100 of them, aged between fourteen and eighteen. Most were at first completely stunned and bewildered by the disasters that had befallen them and their families. First, they had to be taught the fundamentals of politics and the nature of the Weimar Republic and the Third Reich. Calel Lemer was particularly good at this work. He was not only brave and intelligent but also an excellent sportsman and so won them over, and was often regarded as their much loved friend and brother.

To survive prison life morale is vital. Hence we began to organise education and cultural activity. Music, especially singing, means life in prison, and I found that words assumed greater importance than melody in concentration camp songs. We had excellent musicians among us, some who had played in the best European orchestras and fortunately for us there was no ban on musical instruments.

The greatest revelation was choral singing. We had with us one of the best German choral conductors – Rosebery D' Arguto, eventually killed by the SS in Auschwitz in 1943. He was a wonderful musician, had perfect pitch, could produce any note without a tuning fork and was a great enthusiast. My voice was not good enough for singing but I loved listening to the choral rehearsals. He started with a four-part Yiddish song, 'We Used to be Ten Brothers'. It was a sad story of one brother after another dying and both words and melody mirrored our own situation. The choir also sang Schubert's setting of Goethe's 'There was a King in Thule' and settings of poems by Heine. There was also a choir of Czech students in the camp. My cousin, Max Hüttner, was a violinist and used to play to my accompaniment on the guitar.

As we lay on our palliasses at night we gave talks, mainly for the young people. I reproduced what I had learned from Rudolf Israelski in Brandenburg prison about the dialectics of nature and the *Communist Manifesto*, without, of course, referring to Marx and Engels.

On certain occasions we organised evening shows. Some were clandestine, others semi-legal, which meant that permission was obtained but the programme could be changed to something bland and neutral if the SS approached. I recall, for example, such an evening in January 1941. It was to celebrate the birthday of Walter Blass, which coincided with what we called the Three Ls – the customary Lenin, Liebknecht and Luxemburg comme-moration. To deflect attention from our show we arranged a boxing match, which the SS liked to watch, at the other end of the hut. Our evening began with the singing of the Polish revolutionary song, the '*Warszawianka*'. Then the guest of the evening, Ernst Schneller, addressed us. Werner Rosenberg read Erich Weinert's poem '*Proletarische Weihnachten*' ('Prole-tarian Christmas') and I a poem that I had written in prison. The evening concluded with the singing of '*Brüder zur Sonne, zur Freiheit'* ('Brothers Towards the Sun and Freedom'), which, like *'Warszawianka'*, is a revolutionary song translated and sung in many languages).

An important morale-raiser was remembering each other's birthdays. I have already mentioned how I prepared birthday cards. Usually there would also be an extra piece of bread to go with them and perhaps something else besides. I recall that Ernst Schneller found out the day of my own birthday, looked me up in the camp, shook hands and wished me luck in my personal life and in the resistance movement.

For all our efforts to humanise it, Sachsenhausen was and remained a brutal and evil abomination. And yet it also bestowed on me the finest hour of my life. By October 1942 only about 450 of the many thousands of Jewish prisoners brought there were left in the camp, among them some of our most experienced comrades who knew how to interpret and foretell the actions of the administration. On 22 October an order came for Jews not to muster for work. A few hours later the SS came armed with truncheons and in most brutal fashion lined us up in front of the hut. Next, we were marched to the main barrack square where we were made to stand for many hours at two-arms' length from each other. We had to take off our clothes and shoes, stack these neatly in front of us and remain in our underwear and clogs.

The indications were that we were being prepared for liquidation – it was usual to issue only the barest clothes and clogs to those about to be killed. What were we to do? Our group had discussed the situation previously and decided on resistance. There were only ten of us but we knew that some of the young boys would join us. We were marched to the disinfection hut. There we had to strip again and pass three SS men who searched us thoroughly to see that there was nothing hidden on our bodies. The search was accompanied by blows. We assembled again at the other end of the hut. All prisoners were pale, terrified, convinced that their last hour had come. Our small group discussed and decided on our course of action. This had to be so arranged that only we would be attacked and killed. It had to remain only a demonstration. We were not to use Communist slogans in order not to provoke an attack on other Communists in the camp. We decided that when the 12,000 prisoners were assembled on the barrack square we would break out through the window, brush aside the SS guards standing round the hut and run on to the barrack square shouting 'Shoot, you cowards!' to the SS.

We smashed the window. One after another we jumped quickly through the window, a number of the boys came with us and so we were eighteen. The guard at the hut drew his pistol but it was knocked out of his hand. We ran towards the barrack square. We had decided to run along the so-called Lagerstrasse – a wide lane, always empty at roll-calls, which extended from the gate and the watchtower through the camp – so that any shots aimed at us would not hit other prisoners.

There on the square the mass of prisoners stood in silence. Searchlights began to move. Contrary to our expectation the SS officer in charge commanded 'No shooting!' The SS threw themselves at each of us, getting us down to the ground and hitting out with fists and boots. We hit back with all our strength and resisted fiercely. Nothing like it had ever happened in the camps before. The guards with the help of professional criminals were able to subdue us in a few minutes. And as we lay on the ground we were calling out to each other: 'Are you there, Benny? Are you there, Walter? Heads high, comrades! Farewell! To the end!' The SS tried to silence us.

Then complete silence set in for what seemed a very long time, ending with the command of the Camp Commandant – 'Get up.' We got up after one of our comrades repeated the command, lined up correctly and waited for what would happen next. To our surprise the Camp Commandant asked, 'Is anyone of you wounded?' My neighbour whispered that his ribs were broken but we all replied, 'No one is wounded.' 'Where is your footwear?' he asked. 'We left it behind,' we replied.

We were now convinced that we would be led against the camp wall and shot in front of all the assembled prisoners. Instead the Commandant ordered us to return to the disinfection hut and ask for our footwear. He added, 'Don't complicate the already difficult task.' We looked baffled at each other and then one of us issued orders for us to move off. We marched past the columns of prisoners unafraid and proud. On passing the cookhouse we saw our friends through the windows greeting us with raised fists. It was a truly glorious march.

It was difficult to understand why the Commandant behaved in that way. I believe that while we were lying on the ground he had walked up to the disinfection hut where he saw the rest of the 450 prisoners on the ground and the SS beating them with the wooden clogs. He may have concluded that we, eighteen of us, were merely trying to run away from the beating. He had ordered the SS to stop the beating and then returned to the barrack square to deal with us. He had had the order to transfer us out of the camp and wanted to be able to report that all had gone according to plan. We were now issued some thin clothes and clogs, and they returned our pullovers; they also gave us a lump of bread. Then with the rest of the 450 Jewish prisoners we were marched back to the barrack square, where the 12,000 other prisoners were still standing. The same evening we were loaded into freight wagons and began waiting for the train to move.**"**

1. Albert Speer was the Nazi Minister for Armaments; the so-called Speer work squads were run directly by his Ministry rather than the SS or private companies.
2. Besch was a bricklayer and stonemason by trade. A life-long Communist, he served several prison sentences during the Weimar Republic and under the Nazis. He survived the Third Reich, although his spine was injured as a result of torture by the SS and he was confined to a wheelchair towards the end of his life.
3. According to Nazi terminology, *Reichsdeutsche* were 'pure' Germans born within the frontiers of the Third Reich; 'pure' Germans born elsewhere were known as *Volksdeutsche*.
4. The transformation takes its name from the Dutch physicist Henrik-Antoon Lorentz.

7

Auschwitz-Monowitz

Jonny Hüttner and his comrades arrived in Auschwitz on 25 October 1942. Three days later they were stripped and marched single-file past an SS doctor and his orderly who assessed their fitness for work by looking briefly at their muscles, skin, legs and buttocks. Of the 450 new arrivals, 130 were consigned to the gas chambers and the others were taken to the auxiliary camp of Monowitz, where some, including Jonny, remained for the next two years.

Mass murder was the daily routine in all concentration camps. As already mentioned, the Nazis also spoke at times of 'retraining' in the camps, particularly during the early period of the camps' existence, but this was largely a cover-up and, in any case applied only to a few German prisoners. The general policy was to sap the strength of the prisoners by starvation and overwork, and then kill them.

Auschwitz was different. People brought there were examined or, rather, looked at on arrival and killed at once if not judged fit enough for work. Those thus condemned to die included all the elderly, pregnant women and children, as well as the sick and the unfit. The killing was by shooting and injection of phenol into the heart, but mostly by gassing. The gas was Zyklon B, a compound of prussic acid and an inert solid; the lethal gas was liberated when the substance was warmed. The gassing was at first carried out in temporary premises, sealed and adapted for the purpose – a large cellar, two farm houses and the camp morgue. After January 1942, when the Nazis at their so-called Wannsee conference adopted the 'Final Solution', i.e. the murder of all Jews, specially built gas chambers were erected and made to look like shower installations; they were often referred to by the SS as 'saunas'. In them thousands could be and were gassed in a single day. In all, some 4,500,000 people were killed in these ways in Auschwitz. Those selected to die were not registered as prisoners in the camp. The others, 400,000 over the period, were registered, and given individual numbers which were tattooed on their left forearm. Of these 340,000 were to die in the camp from starvation, disease, execution or following subsequent periodic 'selections'. It is scarcely possible to grasp the enormity of human suffering expressed by the above figures and, of course, conversely, the extent of human depravity.

The geographical position of Auschwitz was very convenient to the Nazis. Most of the Jews and Gypsies, whom they intended to kill forthwith, lived in Central Europe. They also planned to exterminate large numbers of Slavs – Poles, Czechs, Ukrainians and Russians – using them first as slave labour and then colonising their lands by 'pure Germans'. Auschwitz was easily accessible from large population centres, such as Warsaw, Cracow, Prague and Vienna, and at the time not within easy reach of Allied bombers. There were coal mines and iron foundries, with a trained workforce in the vicinity. Good land in the area could be used to grow at least some of the food for the SS troops and prisoners. There were also plans to cultivate certain industrial crops, such as *kok-saghys*, which was native to Uzbekistan and thought to contain a workable amount of latex, used in the production of rubber. It is doubtful if the project was ever scientifically valid; it may have been a put up scheme to keep some high-ranking SS officers from front-line service.

The construction of the camp began in May 1940. The work was at first done by German and Polish prisoners. Later, the relative size of the national contingents varied, but the Poles were usually in the majority, especially if Polish Jews are included. Then, for a time, after the outbreak of the war against the Soviet Union, most detainees were Russians, even though large numbers of Soviet prisoners of war were killed on arrival. Others were brought in varying numbers from all countries occupied by the Wehrmacht.

Soon many auxiliary camps sprang up within a hundred kilometres or so of the base – Auschwitz I. The largest and most important was Birkenau, or Auschwitz II, situated three kilometres from the main camp. This was designed to hold 100,000 Soviet prisoners of war, and part of it was assigned for women prisoners. It gained its chief infamy, however, by serving as the extermination centre, and contained the gas chambers and crematoria. The fate of millions of new arrivals was decided and sealed on the railway platform of Auschwitz-Birkenau.

A site seven kilometres from the main camp, at the village of Monowitz, was chosen for the Buna works of one of the largest German industrial concerns – I.G. Farben Industrie. Like three of the company's other plants in Germany it was to be used for the manufacture of synthetic rubber and synthetic fuel. The raw materials – lime and coal – were available locally, and prison labour was to be supplied by the SS, who also employed prisoners of war, forced labour and many civilian workers. (I.G. Farben also produced the Zyklon B gas for the concentration camps.) Prisoners were at first marched the seven kilometres to and from the main camp but this proved unsatisfactory since they would arrive too tired to work well. Rail transport was unreliable, priority being always given to military traffic. It was therefore decided to proceed with the construction of another camp, at the village of Monowitz. This became Auschwitz III, and it sprouted in time more than a dozen subsidiaries. The number of prisoners in the different camps fluctuated. For instance, on 20 January 1944 there were 18,000 in Auschwitz I, 49,000 in Auschwitz II and 6,500 in Monowitz. Later, in August of that year, there were 155,000 in all three camps, of these 35,000 were in Monowitz and its coal mines and factories, with only 10,000 in Monowitz itself.

Utmost overwork, overcrowding with unbearable shortage of air in the huts, primitive sanitation, inadequate diet, frequent 'transfers' (*Überstellungen*) – the Nazi euphemism for post-selection despatch to the gas chambers – and brutal punishments made Monowitz in the unanimous opinion of all survivors, many of whom had already experienced several prisons and concentration camps, the worst of them all. Auschwitz was hell and Monowitz the worst part of it.

The SS resorted to the usual array of punishments, ranging from 'sport', which meant exercises carried on to the total exhaustion of the victims and accompanied by kicks and taunts, to flogging, the withdrawal of part or all of the food, dispatch to the penal company where few remained alive, *Pfahlhängen* or hanging by the wrists, and death by hanging. Another punishment was forcing the individual victims into a square cell in which each wall was just 40 centimetres long and leaving them standing there for hours or days with scarcely any food or water.

That the regime was rigorously enforced was ensured by the Chief Commandant of Auschwitz, Rudolf Höss, who came there from Sachsenhausen bringing with him some of his most brutal assistants. After the war he was handed over to the Polish government, tried in Warsaw, sentenced to death by hanging and taken to Auschwitz for execution.

Monowitz had no gas chambers or crematoria of its own. Those 'selected' were taken to Birkenau. 'Selections' were conducted regularly at the hospital but some prisoners were also picked out for Birkenau during roll-calls on the barrack square, at the Buna works and elsewhere. At irregular intervals, when it was considered necessary to reduce the total population of the camp, a general 'selection' would be arranged.

Himmler and the SS were always ready to feed fresh 'labour fodder' into the jaws of the German war industries, but the managers of I.G. Farben at the Buna works were less than happy at the need to train newcomers every few weeks. They were therefore sometimes open to pleas for a more life-sustaining regime. Twice a week prisoners in certain of their work-squads (*Kommandos*) received two open sandwiches. At one stage the SS brought crematorium equipment to Monowitz but I.G. Farben argued that building the crematorium would lower morale and with it the productivity of the workers. The equipment was removed.

When Auschwitz was being built, in 1940, 1941 and 1942, groups of prisoners were brought there from other camps – Dachau, Buchenwald and Sachsenhausen. These men had had years of prison and concentration camp experience behind them. They were experienced and tempered in the cruel struggle; many were members or even leaders of established resistance groups. Thus resistance came to Auschwitz with the early arrivals. Since in the previous camps the groups were usually made up of people of the same nationality, German, Jewish, Czech, Russian and so on, this was also the case with these new arrivals. This had certain advantages: members of the resistance groups lived and often worked together, had similar problems, knew each other well, and knew who could be trusted and who could not. On the other hand, inter-group understanding and action was difficult and often impossible.

The statistical data on the nationality of the Jewish prisoners are somewhat complicated. Whereas to the Nazis all Jews, irrespective of their country of domicile, were Jews and treated accordingly, some historians, particularly in socialist countries and especially in the German Democratic Republic, do not accept this view and enumerate all prisoners simply by their citizenship or country of origin. Thus Polish Jews are counted as Poles, Hungarian Jews as Hungarians, and so on. This controversial and emotionally charged problem remains unresolved and will not be considered further here.

The largest and most numerous of the resistance groups were Polish. The SS were of course well aware of the fervent patriotism of the Poles as well as their long history of conspiracy. For that reason, and in order to prevent leakage of information about crimes committed in the camp, special measures were taken to insulate it. All civilians who lived within a radius of five kilometres were expelled and their homes either destroyed or handed over to the SS and their families. Forty square kilometres around the camp were declared an exclusion zone: the inhabitants were partially expelled and their place taken by Germans brought from Romania. The only local inhabitants left were miners, railway workers and artisans needed for more skilled work. Nevertheless this insulation was never and could never be complete. Many civilians worked with the prisoners in the factories, and contact could also be made with civilians on temporary work outside the camps.

Polish resistance groups were established chiefly along

political lines. Some were formed by members of the Polish Socialist Party (PPS) and by imprisoned professional army officers. Other groups were of the centre and right-wing parties, and also of the Polish Peasant Party. Likewise, resistance was also political outside the camps. The largest organisation was the right-wing *Armia Krajewa* (Home Army) with its civilian and military wings. The military wing was made up of partisans who organised raids against the Germans, sabotaging railways, power lines and industrial plants. Those in the civilian wing gave all the help they could to prisoners in the camps. Later, detachments were formed of left-wing orientation – *Armia Ludowa* (People's Army), run by the Polish Workers' Party (Communists) and allied organisations. Some prisoners who succeeded in escaping joined one or other of these units. In the clandestine transit of food and medical supplies to the camps, outside resistance groups would often use the same channels, the same intermediaries, regardless of party affiliation, but repeated attempts to establish common action were unsuccessful.

In Monowitz the situation was different from that in Auschwitz I and II. Although the relative size of the national contingents of the prisoners varied at different periods, most were Jews and towards the end between 90 and 95 per cent were Jewish. Many of the leaders of the resistance groups, though coming from different countries, were also Jewish: Stefan Heymann and Kurt Posener of the German group, Julian Barszewski of the French, Arnošt Tauber – the leader of the Czechs – and Oskar Betlen, a Hungarian. Leon Stasiak was leader of the Polish group in the sick-bay. Unlike the position in other camps, co-operation between these mainly Jewish groups in Monowitz was solid. They could indeed be regarded as a single organisation. There were few non-Jewish German prisoners in Monowitz, hence only about a dozen of them were members of the resistance.

Leon Stasiak was generally regarded as one of the most influential men in the resistance organisation. He had been a Communist since his earliest youth and had served prison terms for illegal activity in pre-war Poland. He was in fact in prison at the time the Polish Workers' Party was dissolved and its leaders summoned to Moscow where they disappeared.

Prison probably saved Stasiak. After the German occupation he was arrested, taken to Buchenwald and then transferred to Monowitz in 1942. With four other comrades he managed to escape during the evacuation of the camp in January 1945. They were hidden until the appearance of the Soviet troops by a family, several members of whom were Communists. One of them, Erna, he later married. After the liberation he held important posts in the Polish United Workers' Party. Like many other Jews he was dismissed from his post in 1968.

Oskar Betlen (Bettelheim) was also an experienced and courageous leader. He was born in the Hungarian-speaking part of Slovakia and became a leader of the Slovakian Young Communists. A few weeks after the German occupation of Czechoslovakia he attempted to escape across the Polish frontier but was captured and taken to Buchenwald from where he was transferred to Monowitz in 1942. After the liberation he became a member of the Central Committee of the Hungarian Communist Party and editor of its daily newspaper. Betlen is the author of the best book on the resistance in Monowitz, *Elet a Halál Földjén* ('Life in the Deathfields').

The leader of the German group, Stefan Heymann, was a little older than the other comrades: he was born in Mannheim in 1896. He served in the First World War as an artillery pilot-observer and was severely wounded. After taking part in the short-lived Bavarian revolution he joined the Spartakusbund which later merged with other organisations to form the Communist Party. He soon became a party functionary, and was arrested several times serving a number of prison sentences even before Hitler came to power. After imprisonment he was editor of the party newspaper in Mannheim and a Communist deputy in the Baden parliament. In 1930 he was appointed political editor of the *Rote Fahne*, the party's national daily newspaper. For a few months in 1933 he was the underground leader of the resistance in Silesia. He was arrested and sentenced to two and a half years' imprisonment. Concentration camps followed: Kisslau, Dachau, Buchenwald and, in October 1942, Monowitz. After the evacuation of Monowitz he was transferred to Buchenwald where he was liberated.

In addition to the above groups there were of course many other anti-fascists in the camp, both Jewish and Gentile, Communists and members of other political parties, some of whom held important administrative posts and were thus particularly valuable to the resistance. Many of them were not formally members of the resistance groups but could be approached and asked to co-operate in particular undertakings. They would, on the other hand, often act on their own or initiate useful projects for collective action.

An important non-Jewish personality in the Monowitz resistance movement was Ludwig Wörl, who was for a time the hospital *Älteste*. It was under his direction that the hospital was established and the principal lines of conduct laid down. Wörl was a carpenter by trade and had always been a principled opponent of the Nazis. In 1935 he published and distributed a leaflet entitled *So ist Dachau* in which he described the horrors of that camp. Arrested, he was himself taken to Dachau, thrown into the bunker and kept there nine months, seven of them in chains and in darkness. In 1942 he was transferred to Monowitz and became, as mentioned, hospital *Älteste* being replaced by the more dubious Budziaszek whose role we will discuss later. Wörl employed Jewish doctors, hid weak prisoners and counterfeited selection lists. He stood up to the Nazis by refusing to allow the killing of prisoners by phenol injections while he was hospital *Älteste*.

These men formed the core of the resistance's leadership. Nobody elected them, but their authority, founded on personal example and wisdom, was unchallenged. They and their comrades soon learned that while resistance outside the camps was a way to moral self-preservation, in captivity, for all the hazards, it was also essential for survival.

Soviet prisoners had, according to Hüttner, their own well organised resistance groups. If one includes Jews from formerly Polish territories incorporated into the USSR in 1939, Soviet prisoners constituted one of the largest, if not the largest, national contingent.

The Polish resistance groups in Monowitz were mostly run on nationalist, not to say chauvinist, lines, and co-operation with them was dangerous since many right-wing Poles were at one with the Nazis with regard to Jews and Communists. There were of course also many genuine anti-fascists and internationalists among the Poles, for example Josef Cyrankiewicz, who became later Prime Minister and then President of the Polish People's Republic, and another Socialist functionary, Stanislaw Dubois, who perished in the camp. Some Zionists carried out their own clandestine activities. Attempts to form an international camp committee, such as existed for instance in Buchenwald, were unsuccessful.

In Monowitz, as in most camps, resistance was centred on the hospital. This is understandable. Many hundreds of prisoners converged on it for in-patient and ambulant treatment bringing with them and taking away information to and from the whole camp. They could be spoken to in relative confidence by doctors and orderlies. Members of the resistance could arrange clandestine meetings there more safely than elsewhere. They could circulate between the huts of the hospital by day and, with due precautions, at night. While all the medical work was done by prisoners the person in charge was an SS doctor. He was in some measure interested in efficiency and was therefore open to representation by the staff. And, most important, the hospital cared for thousands of sick and weak people who were in dire need of help and such help was always the main task of the resistance.

The hospital huts did not differ structurally from others in the camp. At times they held up to 1,200 patients. The beds in most of the huts were three-tiered wooden bunks, each of the bunks measuring 180 centimetres by 80 and usually holding two or even three patients. Most of the patients had to be nursed in the bunks. Many suffered from diarrhoea, incontinence and vomiting. There was scarcely any clean linen, clothes were soiled, the smell unbearable. Many were infested, had eczema and scabies. Lack of food and vitamin deficiency favoured development of skin infection and formation of abscesses. Epidemics were frequent, for example, of typhoid and dysentery. Epidemics and sporadic cases of typhus fever also occurred, and of these the SS were greatly frightened. Even a suspicion of the disease would lead to wholesale 'selection' of patients. Prisoners' boots were a constant threat to their health and life. They wore somewhat modified clogs with wooden soles and stiff leather or canvas uppers. These were worn in all kinds of weather, at work and on marches, which could be at the double. They tended to cut into the feet producing badly healing ulcers and abscesses.

The work was exceedingly hard for the weak and undernourished. For example, they had to carry heavy bags of lime and cement. The hours of work were long. Accidents, such as fractures and burns were frequent and implied a virtual sentence of death because patients were not allowed to remain in hospital more than a fortnight. I.G. Farben paid the SS 4 marks a day for the maintenance of trained workers, 3 marks for the untrained, and 1.50 for the sick, the last sum only for a fortnight after which the sick would be 'selected' out. In fact they could be 'selected' after eight days if they had fever, jaundice or any other condition likely to last more than a fortnight.

What the resistance did in certain cases, and that at mortal risk, was to discharge the patients on paper and then readmit them the following day. The SS would be told, if they saw them, that they had been only a day or two in hospital. It had to be made certain, of course, that the visiting SS did not recall the patients on sight and so they had to be hidden at the time of the visit. This was done, for example, in the case of a thirteen year-old boy, Daniel Klowski, who had claimed to be sixteen on arrival at the camp and so escaped initial selection. A wooden box was knocked together for him in which he was carried from hut to hut during the SS inspections. He was treated for empyema and survived. He is now professor of mathematics at the University of Kuibyshev in the USSR. His own story, told twenty years later in the German Democratic Republic in July 1963, at the trial *in absentia* of Hans Globke, one of the authors of the Nürnberg race laws who after the war had been appointed chief of the Chancellor's office under Adenauer in West Germany, is reproduced at the end of this chapter.

At one of the trials, a witness described how those selected were moved to Birkenau. In the beginning ambulances were used, but these held no more than ten people. Then a lorry would draw up in front of the hospital hut. First the corpses would be laid on the floor of the lorry, then the sick would climb up or be heaved up to sit or lie on top of the corpses, at times in several layers.

On arrival at Birkenau the sick were unloaded and taken to the gas chambers. The corpses were cremated, but the capacity of the crematoria was sometimes insufficient, in which case the dead were burned in specially dug trenches or on pyres. The remaining ash was thrown into the neighbouring rivers. Some bones remained unincinerated and these were sent to factories for use as fertiliser.

All the work at the crematoria was done under SS supervision by squads of prisoners, who would also have to remove any gold teeth, dentures, rings and earrings from the corpses. After a certain period these prisoners would themselves be killed so as to eliminate all witnesses to the Nazi deeds.

Experiments on healthy prisoners were conducted in several of the Auschwitz camps but not in Monowitz. At one time an appliance for the administration of electric shocks was constructed by the French-Polish doctor Drohocki and a Dutch prisoner-engineer, Kaplan. The SS doctor in charge, Horst Fischer, became interested in this treatment and applied it to several women whom he regarded as suffering from depression. Whether they were true depressives is doubtful. Some had seen their own children being murdered; one had had her baby snatched from her arms and had witnessed its head being smashed against a wall. However, even though a patient did die during the electric shock treatment as the result of choking on inhaled stomach content, this treatment was not included in the indictment of the doctor when he was tried as a war criminal in 1966.

The career of Dr Fischer is of some interest. He joined the SS as a medical student in 1933 mainly because, as he explained, the uniform made him look more manly. In 1943 he was promoted to be deputy of the chief Auschwitz doctor, Wirths. As such he was, among other things, in medical charge of Monowitz and its outlying camps. Usually accompanied by the NCO, Gerhard Neubert, he did his turn of 'selecting' at Monowitz and elsewhere. He was in attendance at all floggings and executions. He was a mild-mannered man who never shouted and never personally raised his hand against a prisoner. After the evacuation of the camp he met the end of the war as a regimental medical officer in Berlin. Whereas his SS colleagues moved as fast as they could to the west, Fischer reckoned it would be safer for him to remain in the east, where he would be less likely to meet anyone who knew him. He settled with his family in a small town in what later became the GDR and earned a reputation as an esteemed general practitioner. Twenty years later he was, in an undisclosed way, recognised and then tried by the Supreme Court of the Republic. He testified fully and frankly, accepting the guilt of his crimes, was sentenced to death and executed.

Besides the rescue of the sick, a constant and pressing task for members of the resistance was the search for extra food. The prevailing rations were grossly deficient in quantity and quality; nobody could survive on the camp diet longer than three to six months. Some food, and often surprisingly significant amounts of it, was smuggled in by sympathisers outside the camp. Scraps of food remained from the meagre stock brought by those killed on arrival, and some could be purloined from SS stores. Later, parcels of food were sent in on a few occasions by the Polish and International Red Cross, but those receiving them were in a small minority. Part of the scanty rations could be and was sometimes stolen by professional criminals. It was therefore imperative to have reliable comrades on food distribution.

Notifying families of prisoners of the presence in the camp of their relatives was another undertaking. It was also important to record the names of murdered people and those of the Nazi criminals, to let the world know what was happening in the camp.

Attempting to organise the escape of certain prisoners, particularly those in special danger, was another task. This meant preparing food, civilian clothes and establishing contact with partisans or civilians outside the camp. The chances of success were never great. 700 tried it; 400 were recaptured and shot, but some did get away in the confusion of the final camp evacuation.

It was the intention of the SS to break the spirit of the prisoners, to reduce them to a state of mindless hopelessness and apathy. The political work of the resistance was calculated to counteract this by maintaining faith in coming justice and liberation. This was done by spreading news of the advance of the Allied armies. Cultural work, such as songs, talks, clandestine festive occasions and observance of birthdays, was useful in raising morale. An essential task was the placing of trustworthy comrades in key positions. As already mentioned, some of the day-to-day running of the camp was in the hands of prisoner functionaries and some of these were reliable comrades, such, for example, as Ludwig Wörl. On the other hand, where criminals remained at these posts it was sometimes expedient to bribe them. It sometimes even proved possible to persuade the odd SS man to remain neutral or help in some minor way.

In August 1944, as the Soviet army approached Cracow, the SS began to prepare the evacuation of the camp and started to remove all traces of their crimes. Files and archives were burned. The gas chambers and crematoria in Birkenau were blown up. An anxious time set in for members of the resistance groups. They knew that in some camps, for example in Maidanek near Lublin, all prisoners not marched off in time were killed before the entry of the Soviet forces. What were they to do?

Three options were considered: compliance with the evacuation, if that was arranged by the SS, in the hope of flight on the way; break-out before the evacuation; and, lastly, an uprising. An uprising was, of course, a desperate option but preparations for it were taken in hand. Oskar Betlen, who had been a conscript soldier in the Czech army and so became the resistance's only 'military expert', was entrusted with the preparation of the revolt. This he did efficiently, but the plan was reconsidered and abandoned. It was realised that while a dozen or so individuals could possibly escape in the confusion it would mean certain death for the rest of the prisoners.

The departure of the main mass of prisoners, 58,000, took place on 18 January 1945 and proved a tragic event. Many thousands died on the way from exposure, starvation and their escort's bullets, although a few lucky ones managed to escape. About 8,000 prisoners were left in the Auschwitz camps, without food or adequate medical cover. When the Soviet soldiers arrived they found only exhausted, mortally sick or dead prisoners – 600 of them in Monowitz.

* * *

The letter and court testimony which are reproduced below throw light onto the activities of the resistance in Auschwitz. The letter, written in 1964, shows the regard in which Leon Stasiak was held by his comrades in the camp.

My Dear Leon,

This letter will certainly be a surprise for you after so many years. I found out your address from Kurt Posener, to whom I wrote after seeing his own address in a newspaper. Dear Leon, that's how it came about. Now I know that you have a nice wife called Erna and two sons.

Well, about myself. When we marched off from Buna I was told to escape somewhere on the way and look for an address that you gave me, somewhere in Katowice I believe. Somehow this did not work out and so I had to go through another few concentration camps where I nearly perished. Well, with Adi König, Jonny Hüttner and a few others we were together again in camp Dora Mittelbau, Nordhausen, and then taking different routes some of us were liberated on 2 May at Ludwigslust. I went first to my native town, Hanover, to look for my father whom I left behind in Buchenwald in 1942. There I received a message from Stefan Heymann that my father had met his death a few hours before the camp was freed. Initially, on Stefan's advice, I intended to return to Hanover to help in the rebuilding of Germany, but I could not work up any enthusiasm for the idea, and also I found few contacts there. After that I met some old camp comrades and went with them to what was then called Palestine. Now I work at my trade as a gardener and am married; my wife was born in Sanok and we have three children, two daughters and a son. I make a living and am content.

Dear Leon, you would not know me now. I have acquired a

small tummy, am slightly grey-haired and look almost like a petty-bourgeois (*Spiessbürger*). You can't imagine how often we speak about you. My wife and children have known you for many years already. I speak to them, and also to many others, again and again about you, because you were the leading brain in the camp resistance group. Dear Leon, do you still remember Rudi Arndt? The day when he was shot in the Buchenwald quarry, I believe it was the 5th of some month, we wanted to recall it every year. I bear his memory in my heart and expect to cherish it for ever.

Leon, life in the camps is so far away but I relive it constantly and somehow you have become an ideal for me. I was young then, stayed relatively long by your side and so had the chance of being led by a good guide during the formative years in the life of a young man. How I would like to see you again, to swap memories – there are still so many questions to be cleared; you, Leon, held so many threads in your hand. You organised the civilians, made contact with the partisans and also with the other camps. Do you still remember the tubes of toothpaste that I smuggled in to you from the SS hospital in Auschwitz? One of them had a news summary inside written on grease-proof paper? And the messages I had to pass on to Ludwig Wörl in the main camp, as well as others to a woman comrade in the Rajsko camp? Do you also remember Dr Slawa Klein, perhaps you have her address – she was a doctor in Hut 10 in Auschwitz and was one of us. I used to see her regularly, especially when I was on a two month medical orderlies' course in Auschwitz. As you know, I persuaded the chief SS doctor to buy plants in Rajsko and also tools, seeds and so on in other auxiliary camps, so I went to and fro twice a week. This enabled me to maintain contacts and serve as a messenger for you and Oskar Betlen.

Dear Leon, the reason I am rewarming this old brew is that I would much like to know all details of the history of the camp. It is understandable that all our actions at the time were strictly conspiratorial and of course no questions were asked. You and Oskar Betlen could draw on an inexhaustible stock of recollections and show the world that the prisoners were not totally helpless, that though they had no arms they could resist in the most difficult situations and thwart the enemy's wish to destroy us morally.

Dear Leon, how I would like to hear from you! How is Oskar? How indefatigable he was, how indestructible. First, in the typhus fever huts, then in the sick-bay and lastly, when the front approached, forming fighting groups in the huts who were to offer armed resistance if it were to come to the liquidation of the prisoners.

Now about the Auschwitz trial which I have hitherto ignored because it is designed to deal with criminals who are only small, the very smallest of fish. However, somebody did me the doubtful service of citing me as a witness to the Israeli police. I reported to them on the following: Dr König, Dr Fischer and Neubert,[1] and told them about the selections at which the hospital *Älteste*, Dr Budziaszek, co-operated with the Nazis.

As an orderly in the internal diseases department I was present on a number of occasions when Neubert and Budziaszek made lists of people whom they deemed unfit for work. These two creatures wanted to make the lists as long as possible. About Budziaszek we would have a lot to say. Neubert, a very primitive man, was only after personal gain. He would often come to my hut and hold forth on the bodily virtues of the prostitutes in the camp brothel. As you may remember one of my jobs was to collect herbs in the fields and I was ordered to do so in the company of these ladies. On returning from these excursions I would report fully to Neubert on their inner life, giving full vent to my imagination. Now we had a common subject for conversation and he would remind me always of his prowess in this field. But it would also happen that we spoke about the *Muselmanns*, and when in the mood he would give me a full description of the mass murders. Yet he was small fry, unlike Dr Stefan Budziaszek, who was a first class anti-Semite. Well, you knew him better than I did. They asked me also about the other SS NCO Raker. I did not know much about him. Didn't he get you into trouble? But at least he was corrupt and could be bribed.

Dear Leon, *Lamed Wownik*[2] that you were and no doubt still are, think of the times when, in spite of the terror and starvation, we sat together and you initiated me into the teaching of Karl Marx (not much came of it). We sometimes listened to declamation in Yiddish by the actor Palaschinski. I think it was from the play *Night on the Old Market*. I think that I knew you well. You were mostly in a good mood. You did not allow yourself to show anxiety in times of danger but I knew that something was amiss when you bit your nails. So you see, dear Leon, the camp is still in us.

Greetings to your wife and children,

Your friend,

Adi Lindenbaum

Extract from Daniel Klowski's evidence at the trial of Hans Globke, July 1963.

'When the war began I lived with my parents in Grodno. Persecution started on the first day of the occupation. A group of Polish and Jewish members of the intelligentsia were shot. We could no longer walk on the pavements and had to wear yellow stars. The population was enclosed in the ghetto in November 1941. All who attempted to bring goods into the ghetto were shot. The liquidation of the Jewish population began towards the end of 1942; people were sent for extermination to the Treblinka camp.

As a measure of intimidation five people were hanged in the main street of the ghetto, now called Oleg Koshewoy Street. Among them was a young girl. They were left to hang there for three days.

In March 1943 we were taken to the Bialistok ghetto, presumably because the gas chambers at Treblinka were overfilled. On 16 August – it was my birthday – we were told to assemble with a minimum of luggage. That meant extermination ...'

The Judge: 'How old were you at the time?'

Daniel Klowski: 'I was thirteen. Some of the people offered armed resistance. We had to lie down on the ground. The fascists fired over our heads. Among the fascists were also soldiers of the Wehrmacht.

'One day, 150 craftsmen were collected, among them my

father. My mother said, "Stay with your father. Perhaps you will remain alive." That was the last time I saw my mother, sister and younger brother.'

The witness could no longer control his voice. He could resume only after a pause, 'They were probably murdered in Maidanek.'

'At camp Monowitz prisoners worked in the I.G. Farben Buna works. I was very ill at the time. However I met not only beasts but also real people, Communists, members of the resistance, and others. They risked their lives in hiding me for six months because I was very ill and had suppurating wounds.'

The witness could be seen to take deep breaths. Then his voice strengthened and he continued, 'Great help was given to me by the German Communists, Stefan Heymann and Johann Hüttner, the Polish Communists Leon Stasiak and Julian Barszczewski [editor of the Warsaw Yiddish newspaper, *Folkssztime*]. It is difficult for me to express all that these comrades did for me.'

Notes

1. An SS NCO who assisted the SS Dr Fischer in the camp hospital.
2. According to a Jewish legend thirty-six just men, the figure thirty-six written by the letters *lamed* and *wow* in classical Hebrew, are always alive somewhere in the world. They stand up fearlessly to injustice thus ensuring that humanity is never wholly obliterated.

8

Jonny Hüttner in Auschwitz-Monowitz

❝I ended the story of our protest action in Sachsenhausen by telling how, that same evening, we were loaded into cattle trucks and sent off to Auschwitz, though we in fact did not know where we were going. We were given a bread ration and a little margarine, but no water, for the three days journey. Thanks to the presence of experienced comrades there was no panic. Each of us was allowed time to stretch out and sleep. We had no latrine, but prevented fouling of the truck. There were few deaths on the journey.

The train stopped often and long on the way, but at last the heavy doors were noisily pushed aside to shouts of 'Out! Out!' There on the ground stood the SS, whips in hand; lined up, we marched to a stone barrack about a kilometre away.

We did not know then about the mass murder of new arrivals, the gas chambers, but sensed danger around us. They shaved our heads and tattooed numbers on our left forearm. These numbers, unlike earlier ones in other camps, were permanent – to the end. Perhaps this was the end ... The food was much worse than in Sachsenhausen. Things were more chaotic, even the beating was more erratic.

Our first concern was to look for comrades among prisoners already in the camp. A few days earlier a transport like ours had come from Buchenwald. Among the prisoners were members of the German resistance group, Kurt Posener and Stefan Heymann, as well as the Hungarian, Oskar Betlen, and the Pole, Leon Stasiak. They explained to us that a new camp was being built in the vicinity to accommodate prisoner labour for the I.G. Farben Industrie

Buna Works at Monowitz, and that it might be possible to have some reliable comrades appointed there as prisoner functionaries. A few days later, we underwent the first selection and I was among those considered fit for work. We were then marched briskly in columns of 400 to the new location. The ground was irregularly heaped and broken up, there were no proper roads, only a few dirt tracks.

The huts (ours was No.12) were, as in Sachsenhausen, wooden, but they were smaller, each designed for 168 prisoners. There was only one dormitory with three-tiered bunks. A central living space reserved for functionaries contained a few tables and benches. Ordinary prisoners had to sleep, sit and eat on their bunks. There were no lockers. Our clothes, wet or dry, had to be hung up on the bunk posts. The hut had a latrine but no running water or washing facilities. Prisoners had to wash elsewhere, in a specially equipped ablution hut. One blanket and one palliasse were issued for every two prisoners.

I worked at first briefly as an electrician installing electric light in the huts, then was sent road-building – a very difficult job as the soil was heavy clay. The food was terrible. At midday and in the evening we were given thin green soup prepared, they said, from dried vegetables, or leaves, possibly also with some synthetic material. An epidemic of dysentery soon broke out, and in three or four weeks we were all completely exhausted. I was admitted with high fever to the sick-bay. We were fortunate: the hut *Älteste* here was the experienced German Communist, Sepp (Josef) Luger, who did what he could to help us. At that time only a few doctors worked in the sick-bay, most of the work was done by medical orderlies. The doctors were allowed to employ only twenty orderlies to deal with many hundreds of sick people, so some orderlies were kept on unofficially. The 'illegal' orderly would be registered as a patient, discharged on paper after a fortnight and 'readmitted' the following morning.

Ludwig Wörl, who was at the time sick-bay *Älteste*, arranged for me to remain as one of these unofficial orderlies until my position could be legitimised. I joined the work-squad carrying food from the works cookhouse. The squad *Kapo* was a Czech called Hanak, who was a skilled masseur and the

SS liked to be massaged by him. He was, therefore, soon transferred to an auxiliary camp where he could devote more time to massage. I then became a legitimate medical orderly and was put in charge of the carrying of food and its distribution.

It was most important to ensure that the, at best, inadequate food rations were really issued to us and used in the cooking of the soup. With due tact and guile one could also procure a little extra. Later, I was put in charge of the 'tea kitchen' attached to the sick bay. I remained at this post for the whole of my term in Auschwitz-Monowitz. As explained elsewhere, the sick-bay was one of the main centres of clandestine resistance, and I was given different tasks in this connection, and will return to some of them later.

Conditions in the camp were appalling. Overwork, absence of elementary hygienic facilities, insufficient medical attention and severe undernourishment kept average survival down to three months. Yet after 1943 one could perceive some change in the regime. With the advance of the Soviet army and the increasing losses of the Wehrmacht, improved productivity of labour became a pressing need for the Nazis. At Monowitz, I.G. Farben Industrie strove to squeeze as much as possible from each prisoner. Certain arbitrary cruelties, such as wanton beating of prisoners, ceased. This is not to say that the SS, or the professional criminals acting for them, stopped beating or even killing prisoners surreptitiously or when drunk, but such incidents became rare. Punishments, including some of the most inhumane ones, continued, but now only after consideration and by order of the higher SS authorities. The Political Department, i.e. the camp Gestapo, remained very active.

There was cultural activity in the camp. A prisoners' orchestra played cheerful music for prisoners to march out to work and to return to the barrack square, often alas, bringing their sick or dead mates with them. On Sunday afternoons the orchestra gave concerts – in summer on the barrack square, in winter in one of the huts – where there was never enough space for the 'public'. The concerts were very popular, not only with the prisoners but also with the SS. Among the musicians were some excellent soloists who had played with the best European orchestras, and who sometimes gave concerts on their own. My cousin, Max Hüttner, was one of them, and there was also a remarkable Gypsy violinist called Jakob. My cousin said that Jakob was the only Gypsy fiddler he knew who could play with a classical orchestra, and he did so to popular acclaim. On at least one occasion senior SS officers came to listen to him and were visibly moved by his playing.

Another remarkable musician was the singer and virtuoso guitar player Gerd Golinsky. A man of about thirty, he could sing in many languages – Russian, Polish, German, Spanish and Italian among others. He would go from hut to hut singing and playing. I recall a man of about fifty, hopelessly sick and immobile in the top of one of the three-tiered bunks. Golinsky entered and sang a Yiddish song. The old man came suddenly to life, scrambled feebly and clumsily down to the ground and started dancing. He could not be saved, could not recover, but had his moment of happiness. Golinsky was murdered at the Dora concentration camp on the 4th or 5th of April 1945.

Some prisoners played football and there was occasional boxing in the camp, but the few taking part in these sports were 'privileged', being better fed and better clothed.

Like all newcomers in Monowitz the active members of the resistance came from three older camps: Dachau, Buchenwald and Sachsenhausen. To name but a few, including some already mentioned: Ludwig Wörl, Sepp Luger and Schuster from Dachau; Stefan Heymann, Kurt Posener, Ludwig Hess, Leon Stasiak and Oskar Betlen from Buchenwald; Erich Markowitsch, Leo Hauser, Walter Blass, Calel Lemer, Werner Rosenberg, myself, Horst Jonas, Eduard Besch, Hermann Zalka, Jan Grossfeld and Jupp van Snellen from Sachsenhausen. These were joined by Arnošt Tauber from Czechoslovakia and the Austrians, Erich Eisler and Felix Rausch, also transferred from Buchenwald. Most of the above survived and remained in the camp to the end, but Erich Eisler was betrayed and executed.

Our immediate aim was to fill as many of the functionary posts as possible with reliable men. In this we succeeded beyond expectation. Some of our comrades became hut or hall *Ältestes*, clerks, *Kapos*, workers in stores and cookhouses. We had our man as a clerk [*Rapportschreiber*] in the main SS office, one Gustav Herzog, a Viennese, and he had a say in the appointment of hut *Ältestes*. Another comrade, Erwin Schulhof, became chief clerk to the SS *Arbeitsdienst* [the SS officer responsible for all work squads inside and outside the camp]. We even had our people working as interpreters in the Political Department of the camp, and another comrade worked in the camp bunker.

Resistance in the camp consisted, as indicated earlier, of a solidly organised core and a more nebulous periphery of men who could be asked to perform certain tasks or join in selected collective actions. There was, on the other hand, no lack of malevolent types around us – informers, thugs and professional criminals serving as *Kapos* and *Ältestes*. We always had to be on guard. Informers were usually readily unmasked by members of the resistance and their identity did not remain secret from the rest of the prisoners. Since the SS had little appetite for protecting those no longer of use to them, corpses bearing marks of multiple injuries were occasionally found somewhere in the grounds of the camp or the Buna works.

In 1944 we received, hidden in a tube of toothpaste, a circular from the Central Committee of the French Communist Party addressed to party members in prisons, prisoner-of-war camps and concentration camps. It gave guidance on the tasks of the party in such places, stressing particularly the need for national and international solidarity, clandestine propaganda and preparation for escape. We had already acted along similar lines, nevertheless the letter was fully discussed by our committee, accepted and distributed, with appropriate caution, to other camps. I delivered a copy to the women comrades in Rajsko, one of the subsidiary Auschwitz camps.

Some of our men worked as cleaners in the SS huts. One of their tasks was to listen whenever possible to the radio and transmit the news, especially of the Soviet army advances, to Leon Stasiak, who was responsible for its further dissemination. A cleaner named Hermann Zalka was caught with such a bulletin (in Polish) and disaster threatened many of us.

Fortunately, the SS NCO who found the message knew no Polish, could be bribed, and Zalka was not delivered to the Gestapo. Arrangements had to be made, however, for his transfer to another camp. Rather late, in the second half of 1944, contact was made with the Polish Workers' Party and the partisans of the *Armia Ludowa* outside the camp. Thereafter we had regular and reliable bulletins from them.

From time to time transports of new prisoners would be brought directly to Monowitz, bypassing prior selection at Birkenau. One such brought Greek dockers from Salonika. On arrival all their worldly goods were taken from them, some of the valuables going straight into the pockets of the SS, but their own shoes were not removed since it was arranged with the Buna works that carriers of heavy loads would have proper shoes, clogs being a virtual sentence of invalidity. At the disinfection hut, where they went next, however, the men on duty that day were professional criminals who stripped the Greeks of their shoes as well. One of our boys happened to see this and indignantly ran over to tell me about it. We managed to bring this to the notice of the Camp Commandant, Vinzent Schöttl, who ordered that all the Greeks' shoes were to be brought the following morning to the barrack square where their owners could reclaim them.

Deliberate go-slow at construction and manufacture at the Buna works probably had some success, at any rate production there never reached full capacity. Several factors were involved. Parts of the plant that had almost reached manufacturing levels would often be bombed by the Allied air forces, and we thought this was due to intelligence transmitted by the Polish resistance organisation and its partisans. *We* were also asked for details of the Buna works, probably for the Soviet army, and sent off a very detailed plan in which buildings were marked in their order of importance. Some of our comrades delayed construction by sending urgently needed machinery or appliances to departments at a lower stage of readiness, where they could not be immediately used.

A political problem discussed by us in 1944 was the formation by the Nazis of the so-called Dirlewanger SS division, entry into which was encouraged and open to all

German non-Jewish prisoners. There were some comrades who argued that joining it meant getting arms that could be used against the Nazis, but this view was decisively rejected by us following the energetic intervention of the German Communist Emil Meyer. The SS division came thus to be manned almost exclusively by professional criminals with only a sprinkling of anti-fascists. Whether the decision not to join the SS division was right is still being questioned by some of the former prisoners.

The most poignant of my Monowitz experiences arose from the maintenance of contact with comrades in neighbouring camps. This became particularly urgent in 1944 when we began planning for the eventuality of the camp's evacuation by the SS before liberation by the Soviet army. One of these camps was at Rajsko where women prisoners worked in hothouses on practical and experimental horticultural problems. One of our fellow prisoners, Lindenbaum, was a professional gardener and he persuaded the SS to keep buying plants at Rajsko for their gardens. Though reliable, Lindenbaum had been unable to make contact with the Rajsko resistance group. It was therefore decided to send me with him.

We were accompanied by an SS guard. At that time, after the opening in June 1944 of the Second Front in Normandy, many of the German elderly 'home guard' soldiers stationed along the Atlantic became redundant and some were simply put in SS uniforms and posted for duty in concentration camps. Our guard, a former Social Democrat he told us, was one of them and while we were being driven he tried to win our sympathy.

'I am over sixty, and now they have made me wear this uniform,' he said and started crying.

I comforted him by saying, 'One must remain a human being. The uniform is not all that important,' and on reaching Rajsko he took my advice on what to do and what to look for.

As I entered the hothouse a young girl, whom Lindenbaum knew and trusted, asked me what I wanted. I said cautiously that I wanted to meet some German political prisoner who might know someone of my family. Then I waited at the counter pretending to look at the plants and the cards tied to them.

A woman in a white coat appeared and asked, 'You wanted to speak to someone with a political past. Who are you?'

I had to speak about my past in order to gain her confidence and explained that I had been a member of the Young Communist League and had served a term in prison. She decided to test me and asked, 'Where are you from?'

'Berlin.'

'What can you tell me about the district you lived in?' And then suddenly: 'Do you know the agitprop troupe *Das rote Sprachrohr*?'

'Very well,' I said, surprised at her question.

'Then give me some names.'

I named Maxim and Edith Vallentin, Gerda Sandberg, my sister and myself. Her eyes grew larger and larger and we recognised each other: she was Elli Schliesser, one of the leaders of the *Rotes Sprachrohr*. We had changed, our faces were different; it was ten years, and what years, since we last met. I ran and embraced her. What joy!

Then she looked at me, 'What do you want?'

I was wearing my well-fitting medical uniform and was rather well dressed for a prisoner with a white made-to-measure tunic and a smart well-set cap.

'Who are you now?' she asked.

I explained. She asked me to wait. She had to discuss me and my proposition with members of her group – French and Czech chemists and biologists. Then she returned saying, 'You must understand that we must have proof of your reliability. I knew you as a good comrade but it was many years ago. We must start again.' And she gave me a task: 'In Birkenau a group of French women comrades have been sent to the penal company. They are in a work squad loading wagonettes, on reduced rations and are certain to perish unless rescued in time. If you can manage to help them through your organisation we shall trust you!' I accepted the challenge, returned to Monowitz and discussed the problem with Stasiak and Heymann. We had a contact in Birkenau – a former International Brigader, now unfortunately demoralised and unreliable, who drank with the SS. But we could appeal to his conscience and did so. He helped, and we succeeded in freeing the ten women from the penal company.

The last year of Monowitz, 1944, presented us with two major new problems. The Germans occupied Hungary and embarked on the extermination of its Jewish population; if they could not win the war they could at least murder all Jews. Large numbers of Hungarians (400,000 in the course of a few months) and of Greeks began to arrive at Auschwitz. Most went straight to the gas chambers in Birkenau but many were also brought to Monowitz and it was up to us to teach them how to survive. The second and even more worrying problem was the fate of us all before liberation.

It was generally believed that few, if any, prisoners would be left alive to be freed by the Soviet army. Several contingencies had therefore to be foreseen. We began to consider a possible uprising and formed groups of future fighters. This work proceeded quite successfully. Preparations were also made for the escape of certain comrades. All this had to be kept strictly secret and only participants were informed of their own planned roles. My task was to collect and store empty soda water bottles which we intended to fill with sand and use as missiles against the SS. A surprise attack might have given us a much needed start of a minute or two. I did in fact collect and store a few hundred of these bottles. In the event, these preparations were suspended by the decision of the committee.

Another very dangerous step was to send anonymous letters to the Camp Commandant and to Dr Fischer in which they were told that if they abstained from further killing of prisoners a good word would be put in for them after the German defeat. The letters were typed by Arnošt Tauber on a typewriter in one of the Buna works offices. When they were received the Gestapo instigated a most determined search for the typewriter, and did in the end find it – on one of the scrap heaps of the works. They were told that it had been thrown out months earlier, so anyone could have used it. Actually, it was carefully damaged and thrown out only two days earlier. Tauber and with him many of us were saved, but it was a close thing.

The new Soviet army offensive from Baranow, about fifty kilometres from Auschwitz, began in January 1945, and all work in the camp came to a halt on the 17th of the month. At 8 a.m. on the 18th we were formed up in columns and set to march towards Gleiwitz, sixty kilometres to the west. It was bitterly cold, between −15 and −20 degrees centigrade at night. The march was brisk. Stragglers were immediately shot and left by the wayside. We reached the halfway halt, at Mikolay, by nightfall and had a few hours rest in an unheated barn. Escape on the way was not planned although there were dense woods alongside and it would have been possible. I was instructed by Stasiak to remain with the French group since many of them could not speak German.

Next day we marched on to Gleiwitz, the location of two auxiliary concentration camps. These were designed to hold 2,000 prisoners but now contained 10,000 with more constantly arriving. After three days we were loaded onto open high-sided freight trucks used for carrying coal, lumps of which were still frozen to the floor. Our French group managed to stay together in one of the trucks. On leaving Auschwitz we were able to take as many clothes as we could carry because much of the stored material was being abandoned. Nevertheless many prisoners froze to death. Of 4,000 on our train about 1,300 died. In Gleiwitz we were issued 300 grammes of bread and some tinned meat. We also had obtained some vitamin tablets.

For nine days we travelled through Czechoslovakia and Germany, with only one further issue of food, on the fourth day. We had no water and collected snow as it fell in our tunics. We managed to control all incipient quarrels and fights, shared out food equally and insisted that all urinated outside the truck. Discipline and order were strictly maintained and no one gained at the expense of another. There were no deaths among members of our resistance group and fewer deaths of other prisoners in our truck than in any of the others. Despite being moved to another truck, as ours was designated for storing corpses after the railway authorities complained about corpses being thrown off the train, we managed to stay together.

On the ninth day we stopped at a strange built-up area and

were ordered down. All of us were exceedingly weak but I was picked as one of those who had to unload the corpses which were frozen to one another and to the truck, a devilish job made even worse by my hardly being able to stand on my feet.

Many chimney-like shafts protruded from the ground; they were, as we discovered, ventilation shafts. We did not know where we were. It was the concentration camp of Mittelbau Dora.**99**

9

Mittelbau Dora and the Flying Bomb Factory

On the night of the 17-18 of August 1943, 433 RAF bombers raided Peenemünde where the German V weapons, the V1 flying bomb and the V2 rocket, were being manufactured. The damage was crippling and further work was suspended. A search was set afoot for underground caves or man-made galleries suitable for conversion to bomb-proof factories. One such site was found near the small town of Nordhausen, now in the GDR, at the eastern foothills of the Harz mountains, about thirty kilometres from the present West German frontier.

A subterranean complex of caves, tunnels and galleries had been built there long before the war for the safe and secret storage of war materials, poison gas and sulphuric acid. Two tunnels ran north to south for 1,800 metres. Fifty galleries opened at right angles to the tunnels, some ending blindly and others connecting the two parallel tunnels. The galleries were 200 metres long, 8.5 metres high and 12.5 metres wide. In accordance with the usual German practice of the time the same components of the rockets were built simultaneously at two other sites: Wiener Neustadt in Austria and Friedrichshafen on the Rhine, while some parts were also manufactured in Riga. The overall responsibility for the project was held by the Minister of Armaments, Albert Speer; scientific and technical organisation was in the hands of Wernher von Braun.

The code name given to the project was Dora and the works with the concentration camp came to be known as Mittelbau Dora.

Adaptation of the galleries began in August 1943. The work was done by groups of prisoners brought seriatim from neighbouring Buchenwald and then from other camps as well as directly after their arrest. Living and working conditions in the galleries were horrendous. There was of course no daylight and only the dimmest artificial light. Dust from the drilling was thick in the air and on the ground. There were no sanitary facilities. A few large tents stood close to the entrance of the tunnels but sufficed for only a small number of prisoners, the rest slept and lived in the galleries, on the rock face. Later, four-tiered bunks were installed in two of the galleries. Prisoners were kept underground for weeks on end, working twelve to fourteen hours a day. As the population grew, the usual camp huts were erected in the open country adjacent to the galleries with the customary services: barrack square, bunker, crematorium and so on. Although there were improvements, as many as 20,000 of the total of some 60,000 prisoners brought to Mittelbau Dora perished in the appalling conditions. In January 1944 some 7,000 prisoners still lived underground.

Initially a subsidiary of Buchenwald, Dora became administratively independent in October 1944. It acquired its own auxiliary camps in the neighbourhood, one of which was located in the town of Nordhausen itself. It was placed in the suburb called Boelcke and consisted of two enormous hangar-like garages, built for tanks on the ground level, with living space for their crews on two higher levels. The camp authorities used it as a kind of sick-bay to house prisoners no longer fit for work prior to dispatching them for liquidation to Bergen-Belsen.

It is believed that to preserve complete secrecy it was Hitler's wish that only Germans be employed in the camp, but this proved unrealistic. The alternative was that no one should ever be released from the camp. New arrivals came from twenty-one different countries. Most were Soviet people – a total of 9,481, then Poles, French, Germans, Belgians and the others. After Italy's capitulation, Italian soldiers falling into the hands of the Republican (Mussolini's) army or the German Wehrmacht were treated as prisoners of war and forced to work in the galleries. Some of them protested, whereupon the SS summarily shot seven of their officers.

In addition to the V1 and V2, other military objects were manufactured in the galleries – fighter planes, surface-to-air-missiles, liquid oxygen and motor fuel. Albert Speer's Ministry planned to make Mittelbau Dora the largest underground factory complex in Europe. Many civilians were also employed in the works as engineers, draughtsmen, and others. Some came as forced or directed labour, others were volunteers. Prisoners of war, like the unfortunate Italians mentioned above, were likewise set to work in the galleries.

The plan was to produce 12,000 V2s in thirteen months, but only 6,000 were assembled in twelve months, and many of these were faulty. Some would explode on testing, others would not start, explode on the launching platforms, or not reach the target. According to two British historians, London was hit 517 times and the rest of England 537 times.[1] It may well be assumed that some of the rockets aimed at London fell into the sea, and that some of the others listed as having fallen in 'the rest of England' had also been aimed at London. Another much suffering city was Antwerp, hit 1,265 times.

Among the earliest newcomers to the camp were also organisers of resistance. Most were experienced Communist Party members, such as their leader, Albert Kuntz, an alternate member of the Communist Party Central Committee and erstwhile deputy of the Prussian Landtag (parliament). Some foreign prisoners also took part in the resistance. Among the latter was the Czech doctor Jan Cespiva, remembered for his humanity and courage.

As in other camps, the main objective of the resistance was mutual aid. As elsewhere, it proved possible to place reliable men in influential prisoner-functionary posts. Moreover, in view of the decisive military role ascribed by the Nazis to the V weapons, sabotage of production assumed special importance. Efforts were made to disrupt production at minimum human cost. It was attempted to work as slowly as possible, to delay the dispatch and transport of essential components, to assemble these incorrectly and to misconnect wires in the rockets' electrical circuits. It is difficult to estimate how effective all this proved to be, but the high rate of rocket failures alerted the SS to the possibility of sabotage and agents of their SD (SS security service) were planted in the galleries. Intimidation and terror became the order of the day. The sight of individuals or groups of victims hanged from jibs and gantries at the entrance to the tunnels met the prisoners on their way to work. Informers were set to spy out the anti-fascists. Many activists were arrested, thrown into the bunker and tortured before execution, among them Albert Kuntz, who was beaten to death on 22 January 1945.

When the Allied armies approached the camp the Nazis decided to send the scientific and technical leaders to the Alps; prisoners were to be transferred to other camps. On 4 April 1945 Nordhausen was heavily bombed and 1,300 prisoners perished in the raid. Evacuation of prisoners to Mauthausen, Sachsenhausen, Bergen-Belsen and other camps followed, and was conducted with chaotic cruelty which was, perhaps, even worse than the usual. Over 1,000 prisoners were locked in a barn which was set on fire the next day. One of the victims, as already related, was Calel Lemer.

American troops entering the camp on the 11 April found 680 sick and dying people and many corpses. Advance troops were followed rapidly by detachments of civil and military intelligence. All rockets and installations were removed and taken away. Even more valuable for them was Wernher von Braun himself, captured with his colleagues in the Bavarian Alps. These particular prisoners were more than fortunate. Instead of having to face military tribunals for war crimes, they were taken to the USA where in the course of time they were able to gain the highest rewards and honours that country could bestow.

In accordance with the Yalta agreement, concluded in February 1945, the Americans left the area on 1 July and it was taken over by the Soviet army. In the ensuing summer galleries were blown up and the entrances to the main tunnels solidly blocked up. Like some other concentration camps, Dora was in time converted into a Place of Remembrance and Warning.

Some present-day visitors may feel the incongruity of the beautiful countryside and the grim story of the place. They

Jürgen von Woyski's monument at Mittelbau Dora

will find a well-arranged memorial, a few models of the rockets, the barrack square, the crematorium and a museum displaying among other exhibits, photographs of some of the resistance heroes. Most of the portraits seem to be enlargements of something like passport photographs and the faces are hence stiff and lifeless. As mentioned, the entrances to the tunnels have been blocked and are now totally overgrown. At the foot of the Kohnstein mountain stands a monument to the fallen. The sculptor, Jürgen von Woyski, has created a group of gaunt and resolute men. Such men never ceased to believe in ultimate liberation, worked for it and offered all resistance possible under the cruellest of circumstances. Those who survived embarked on the daunting but rewarding task of building a new Germany in which fascism could not recur. Streams of visitors, especially the young, come to pay homage and to lay fresh flowers at the feet of the figures.

Notes

1. Peter Calvocoressi and Guy Wint, *In Total War*, Harmondsworth 1974, p.525.

10

Jonny Hüttner in Mittelbau Dora

66After the unloading, and despite extreme weakness, I managed to carry about a dozen frozen corpses and then rejoined our group. We were taken to be disinfected and washed. We had to step into a large container filled with disinfectant and duck below the surface of the solution. Then, under the showers, we drank our fill of warm water, the first real water in eight days. However, the bliss of drinking was spoilt for me by the loss of my shoes. Shoes were our most treasured possession and we hung on to them like grim death.

As I stood under the shower I held my shoes under my arm. Suddenly I felt one of them being pulled out by someone behind me. Turning I could still see the thief and as I bolted after him the second shoe was pulled out. Chasing the second thief I saw him vanish into a small shack and there at the door stood a man with a bared knife in his hand. He was, by the marking on his tunic (a green triangle), a professional criminal. I found out later that they were a well known gang in the camp, the leader sending out boys of fourteen and fifteen to rob newcomers. The stolen articles were traded for such items as bread or margarine. At the time I was naked and helpless and my good shoes were gone. I was given another pair, old and torn, with a cleft between the sole and the uppers. They weren't even a match: the left was a size or two larger than the right. I knew from past experience how worse than useless it was to complain to the SS or anybody else. The loss had to be accepted.

After the showers we were taken to our hut with the

customary three-tiered bunks and a palliasse and blanket for two. Not really two: prisoners in the Dora camp worked twelve-hour shifts and the same bunk, blanket and palliasse were shared by pairs on both shifts. All this, however worrying to prisoners new to a concentration camp, was more or less routine to us. We were left to rest for three days and then put to work.

I was sent to carry bottle-shaped metal tubes, holding these under both arms. Ours was a squad of some fifty and a *Kapo*. The load had to be taken into a tunnel, and what a tunnel … Ten steps in and it was dark, one hardly saw anything. It was a kilometre long. We had to deposit the tubes at a certain spot, return empty-handed and then keep repeating the round for twelve hours. Many broke down under the strain.

The earliest need was to find comrades scattered through the camp and consider further plans. In my own hut I found Victor Malik, a member of the French group and an old friend of mine who had been with us in Auschwitz.

After a week or two it was announced that a clerk was needed somewhere in the works. I knew nothing then of the V bombs. A clerk was sought, so I stepped forward saying, 'I am a clerk.' When asked where I had worked, I replied that I had been employed by the Deutsche Bank and the Diskonto Gesellschaft. This was a half-truth. I had worked only in the second of the two banks for a short time after leaving primary school, but I wanted to find easier work and I got the job.

My work station was in a gallery shed knocked together out of rough boards. I had to keep a file of certain items in stock, order new ones when we ran short of them, and issue these on demand. Among the items were metal bottles, five of which had to be inserted together into a seamless metal cylinder to form a 'battery'. These batteries were tested to withstand fifty atmospheres of pressure. I was told that in the V2s the pressure would be twenty-five atmospheres. What the substance was they put in the bottles I never found out. By mistake I once used a seamed rather than a seamless cylinder and it came apart on testing. This gave me the idea of doing it on purpose, hoping that it would remain unnoticed, and I did so when I could.

I got to know a Dutchman who worked in von Braun's office. He was a patriot but not a socialist. At his work he could hear the radio and would bring me daily reports of the American troops' advances. When the Americans came within twenty kilometres of Nordhausen he would come in several times a day to give me the latest positions.

With me in the makeshift office worked two German civilians, one a university-trained engineer and the other a technician. They were what was known as *dienstverpflichtet* [directed to certain work] and I soon discovered that they were not unfriendly towards me. One was a man from Dresden and he came back after three days' leave in that city shaken to the core. He sat at the table head down, pale, supporting himself with both arms, hardly able to work. Something terrible must have happened to him or his family, perhaps in the air raid on Dresden. The other civilian returned in a similar state from his home city, Magdeburg. They never mentioned the bombing – they were also *schweigeverpflichtet* [sworn to secrecy]. However, I did find out from them how large Dora really was. Whole trains could traverse the tunnels. They also left bread for me which at first I did not touch because it was kept in a locker. Then one of them exclaimed aloud, 'Look, look, the bread is still here,' and I knew that I was to have it. It was a daring act on their part; had they been discovered by the SS they would have been put in prisoners' clothes and treated like the rest of us.

I was still very weak but as clerk had a relatively easy time. I saw how other prisoners were exploited and maltreated. Almost totally exhausted men, they were Hungarian Jews, carried heavy containers past our shed, eight men to a container. They swayed, their legs would give way while an SS man walked alongside and kept beating them as hard as he could. I can't think what moved me, perhaps it was because I felt feverish and could watch the torture no longer, but I turned to the SS man and said, 'What is the use of beating them? They can hardly stand.' I stood rigidly at attention, as I had to when speaking to the SS, and stared at him firmly. The two civilians were watching, and he did not hit me. Any other time, when fully accountable, I would not have dared to speak like that, and if I had he would have surely beaten me to death.

In February and March 1945, the SS started on multiple

executions at the entrance and exit to Tunnel B. The victims, mostly young Soviet men, were hanged for alleged sabotage. They were strangled by a wire noose and to frighten the rest of us left hanging from jibs and gantries. Two or three prisoners were hanged daily. The civilians in my office explained that, according to plan, fifty V2s were to be produced daily, but the actual figure was twenty-five, and only half of these were usable. Hence the Gestapo were called in and started their searches, arresting, torturing and murdering people. I felt that the civilians were worried and tried to warn me. The Gestapo were closing in on our part of the works. They had noticed perhaps that I was erratic in my ordering, asking for too many of some components and too few of others. I discussed the position with my friend Victor Malik and with other comrades and we all thought that it was time for me to quit the galleries.

I had an idea: the SS doctor, Orthmann, who treated me once in Sachsenhausen, was now working here. I composed a letter in which I thanked him for the help he gave me when I broke my leg in Sachsenhausen and offered my services now as a medical orderly. We had a contact in the sick-bay, Adi Lindenbaum, and I gave him the letter which he pushed under the door to Dr Orthmann's consulting room. It was of course a dangerous thing to do, but with the gallows looming one had to take risks, and it came off. That same day I was called to see the doctor. He asked me about my confinement in the concentration camps. I did not tell him about my term in prison, saying merely that I was now seven years in the camps as a Jew, and asked to be employed as an orderly. Another prisoner whom I did not know was present at the interview. He was Orthmann's clerk and happened to be a good comrade, an Austrian, I believe. Orthmann glanced at him in a sort of prompting way as if suggesting that he should do something for me. The clerk said that it would be best for me to go to Nordhausen, the auxiliary camp for unfit prisoners, where I could work in the sick bay.

I cannot explain why Dr Orthmann decided to help me. He was an SS officer, worked in concentration camps and as such would certainly have had to stand trial after the war. That fate he avoided by shooting himself when the camp was liberated.

A little later I was summoned to the camp office and the clerks there looked at me with overt suspicion. After I had explained everything to them their attitude changed. They realised that I merely wanted to get out of the galleries and was no kind of collaborator or informer. They arranged for me to join a group of prisoners sent that day to Nordhausen, four kilometres south of the Dora camp.

On arrival we were met by an SS NCO and several comrades whom I knew from Monowitz. I jumped off the lorry in a sprightly fashion to show them that unlike the others I was fit for work. Standing to attention I reported to the SS NCO stating my name and number, then stepped over to the sick-bay *Älteste*, a good comrade from Monowitz, who told the SS man, 'Yes, this is our man. We need him in the sick-bay.'

The Boelcke barracks were old tank hangars, and now held 2,000 prisoners. They were equipped with heavy iron gates and with a wall and fences round the entire site, but no electrified barbed wire. The fences were rather makeshift and the wooden watchtower seemed to be similarly imperfectly made.

One of our people who worked in the cookhouse managed to find me a little extra food and in four days I felt much stronger and able to work. My job was to collect food in the cookhouse and hand it out to the prisoners in my dormitory. There were 500 of them, all unfit for work. Many suffered from typhus fever, all were lousy. New arrivals were no longer being deloused and disinfected. Everything was now slipshod, and seemed to be in a state of decay, as indeed it was. My job, involving constant circulation between cookhouse and barracks, allowed me to meet contacts and we soon established a closely knit resistance group. Most were French, with a few Germans like myself.

On 3 April Nordhausen and the Boelcke barracks were heavily bombed. One of our barrack gates and also part of the stone wall and the fence were demolished. Instinctively, I and a German comrade, Ludwig Hess, ran about 300 metres out of camp and fell flat into a bomb crater. Ludwig Hess had a bad hip and could not run fast. When the raid was over we got up prepared to run farther to the nearby wood. But above us stood an SS man with a drawn revolver. By chance he happened to be a driver I knew in Monowitz who used to drive people to the gas chambers in Birkenau. I straightened up and reported smartly, 'Two prisoners, so and so, sheltering from the enemy terror raid.' He may have recognised me or my mate and put away his gun, 'Well, you are lucky that it was me, anyone else would have shot you! Now, march back to camp!' And we returned.

That afternoon we discussed the situation with nine other comrades and the eleven of us agreed on escape should the air raid be repeated. Our past experience was that raids recurred at exactly the same time of day. We therefore embarked on a more thorough preparation for the escape. We managed to obtain some food. At that time some of us, including myself, wore modified civilian clothes. The striped drilling was now in short supply and the SS fitted out prisoners with suits taken from those they had gassed. The back of the jacket had a painted cross or sewn-in patch of striped fabric and a similar patch was sewn in on one of the trouser legs. We therefore decided to wind a rolled blanket diagonally, as soldiers did, around our jackets, and to carry something in our hand to cover the patch on the trouser leg – all this to try and look like ordinary civilians, thousands of whom were running out of the town before and during the bombing. And we firmly resolved to run and run as long as the bombs fell. The guards would be in their shelters, in trenches or lying flat on the ground. Were we caught we would certainly be shot.**"**

11
Escape and Freedom

❝The following day, at exactly the time we had anticipated, the sirens started wailing, the guards took shelter and we wound the blankets around us. Then we ran out through the smashed gate and the gap in the camp wall into the open where I gave the command to lie down and wait for the bombs. When the planes were over us I shouted, 'Up and run!'

As on the previous day, the raid was terrifying. The Allies must have found out that the V2s were being manufactured at or near Nordhausen. The underground galleries were, of course, bomb-proof, but 80 per cent of the town was destroyed, thousands of the inhabitants killed, and with them 500 prisoners. As the bombs fell the noise was deafening. The air was full of the whine of bombs, whistling bullets and shrapnel. The earth heaved and rolled under us. We ran, and with us ran thousands of civilians who were also seeking safety in the woods. Suddenly there came a spell of even more overwhelming bombing and we fell and flattened ourselves in a ditch. For a moment I felt like staying there but remembered at once that we had to run.

I shook the comrades by the shoulder and shouted but they were numb with fear, paralysed. I had to run alone and did so. I had to cross a major road, and in the gutters along it lay armed soldiers who shouted at me to lie down. This would have been fatal, however, and with all my strength I leaped over them and into the wood on the other side of the road. 100 metres or so into the wood, I stopped and looked round. There was no sign of my companions and I prowled round till I came to a hamlet, which I think was called Uthleben.

It was getting dark. I was dead tired and began looking around for a place to spend the night when I saw a farmstead with a barn. That barn would have been the right place but its gate was locked. Going round the house I found a kind of narrow staircase leading to the loft and went up. I entered through an unlocked door and found corn strewn on the floor and decided to sleep right there. There was little else I could do; the mental and physical stress of the day had been enormous and I was now dead beat and cold. So I fell asleep in the corner of the attic but woke during the night to relieve myself. I intended to slip stealthily downstairs but to my alarm found the door locked. Someone must have seen me and locked the door. I had to empty my bladder indoors and hated doing so. In trying to open the door I noticed that soldiers were quartered in the house. The problem was how to get out. It was impossible to use the hatch which was too high off the ground to jump down from. I fell asleep again to wake with the morning grey. On trying the door again I found that it was now open. Soldiers were going about their business down below. Now, I thought, I was in a trap, but there was nothing for it and I went, looking purposeful, down the staircase and around the house. Nobody stopped me.

On the morning of my second day of freedom I was back in the woods and weaving my way westwards when I glimpsed a man through the foliage darting from cover to cover. When he noticed me he tried to hide behind a tree. This and other signs – it seemed to me that he was wearing the striped prisoners' uniform – indicated that he was also an escaper. I stepped forward and hailed him. He, in his turn, recalled seeing me somewhere in Auschwitz. He was a French doctor whose name I do not recall. He understood German and could speak the language, though not very well. We agreed to join up and walk together, remaining well inside the forest and making sure that no one was about before running across a clearing. In this way we covered many kilometres, guided by the sun, though as it was not always visible we must at times have walked in circles.

It was getting dark when we spotted a party of men

working in a field by the forest. They wore tattered French uniforms at which my companion grew very agitated. We approached stealthily and, seeing no guards, called out. The men came over but were also very cautious. After some discussion it was agreed that we would stay in the wood till complete darkness when someone would fetch us.

We waited some hours for the guide and were then taken to a cowshed which served also as the billet for the men, who were French prisoners-of-war. The farm was on the outskirts of a village called Bleicherode. That night we slept with the men (and the cows) in the cowshed. Some of our hosts spoke German and asked me searching questions, wanting to make sure that I was a *bona fide* anti-fascist and not some kind of collaborator. I showed them the tattooed number on my forearm and told them that I was a member of the Communist Party; two of them also admitted to being Communists. We discussed our escape. My companion presented no problem. They fitted him out with civilian clothes and identity papers, even letters from his assumed family in France, and he could thus pass credibly for a civilian French worker. I, however, spoke no French and they could provide me with no papers. They could do little for me but adjust my civilian clothes better to conceal the tell-tale prisoner patches and cover up my tattoo with a plaster, making me less recognisably an escaper.

It was decided that we should stay another day and night with them to await the regular prisoner-of-war courier due to bring mail for them. He would guide us to the next station, a place called Himmelpforte which, not inappropriately, means gate of heaven. The mail was being sorted out and distributed from the main prisoner-of-war camp which was also the centre for the allocation of men for work at various farms in the area, including the one at Bleicherode.

The courier duly arrived and at about five in the morning took us at a brisk pace over precipitous paths to Himmelpforte. The Frenchmen there were unfriendly. They resented me, a German, being foisted on them and treated me with undisguised contempt. They wanted to get rid of both of us as soon as possible and decided to send us off the same day to the main camp which was, they said, already under the control of the International Red Cross.

I don't know who these people were. They wore civilian clothes and could have been volunteer workers who came to Germany because conditions, and particularly the food, were better than in occupied France. I did not openly oppose the plan but made up my mind to stay away from any prisoner-of-war camp.

We left Himmelpforte in the afternoon and as soon as we were out of sight I explained to the doctor that I was now free for the first time in nine years and that every extra day of freedom was a bonus.

'You go your way and I shall follow mine,' I said. We parted. He went east to the camp and I went west. Already in Dora I had known approximately where the American lines lay, and, hoping that they were not very far, strode more confidently until I came to a farmstead with a barn. The barn was open and, thoroughly exhausted, I lay down in it by the door. At about six o'clock in the morning, I was wakened by a slight rustle. A girl, about sixteen years old, was standing there and handed me a thick slice of bread generously spread with lard. Someone in the farm must have seen me entering and sent the girl with the food. Not a word passed, but I was all but overcome by the magic of the moment – someone so unexpectedly sending out bread to an escaper.

I slipped out cautiously so as not to be seen and thus endanger the good farm people, reached the forest and again went westward by the sun. At one point I came up against a steep rocky hill and had to follow a path hewn half-way up its slope, where it curved eastwards.

Suddenly I was faced by two men blocking the way. They wore civilian clothes but had military belts with guns in their holsters. They must have been SD men [the SS security service] who were then being stationed behind all German fronts to intercept and deal with deserters.

'Halt! Hands up!' they commanded. 'Where are you from?'

I answered in broken German with an assumed French accent, 'Come from Nordhausen.'

'Where are you going?' Not able to think of any other place, I said Bleicherode, still with a French accent. 'My brother Bleicherode. I ... my brother.'

'Your papers.'

I had, of course, no papers and so went on, 'Nordhausen all *kaputt*. Bombs, *kaputt*. I … my brother.'

One of them started fingering his holster, but at that moment a shrill whistle came from the farm below and I saw a man signalling to them to hurry down. They threw angry glances at me but went down as ordered. With my heart hammering I continued steadily along the path, now downwards.

At the bottom of the path stood a peasant with a pitch-fork in his hand who started asking me where I was from and where was I going. I answered as I had the men above – I could trust no one. He said that he would come with me.

'But I want to Bleicherode,' I said.

'Bleicherode is the other way,' he said, 'You have passed Bleicherode. But I will show you something.'

After walking about 300 metres he pointed to a coppice on the crest of the hills about ten kilometres away. 'The Americans are there,' he said.

I pretended not to be interested and said, 'Yes, yes. Then Bleicherode, I go back and left, you said.'

He left me, and I crouched for a while behind the trees to watch what he might be up to, but he went on his way. He must have been a decent man and he had really wanted to help me. I wondered who he was – tall and robust – and why was he not in the Wehrmacht.

Then I began walking towards the hills, steadily westward. I went through a forest and the world became enchanted. The fresh spring leaves glowed and sparkled with the sun's rays breaking through the trees. I had never seen anything like it.

It took me about two hours to reach the spot indicated by the man below. I found myself at the outskirts of a village. I did not know its name but found out later that it was Holz-thaleben. As I walked along the edge of the wood I was suddenly startled by the sound of rifle locks being reloaded. It must have been pickets stationed in haystacks on the outskirts of the village. All I could do was to proceed as calmly as possible. Had I tried to slip back into the wood I might have been shot at. I had to pretend to be a civilian going about his business and walked along a road leading into the village, on both sides of which stood large tanks.

I passed these without being taken notice of and thought to myself, 'Good God – I have had police arresting me, the Gestapo, the SS, the SD, the Wehrmacht and now also tanks,' and walked on looking neither left nor right. Out of the corner of my eyes I saw men in camouflaged overalls opening tins of food. They ignored me.

At the first houses in the village stood a man holding a milk can. He stepped in front of me and asked where I came from. I replied, 'Nordhausen.'

He went on, 'Do you know where you are?' and I answered that I did not know the name of the village and had seen no signpost either. He said, 'The village is occupied by the Americans. Look, these are their tanks with the white star on them.'

I did not quite believe him, but he went on, 'Look, look at their uniforms!'

I looked more openly, went up to the tanks, saw the crews eating and smoking. I turned to one of them with a few words of my rudimentary English but he showed no interest whatever. I felt brimful with joy, free, liberated. The man with the milk can watched me, and when I returned to him said that it would be best for me to go to the commandant. He pointed out the house in which, he said, the commandant worked on the ground floor.

I entered the room and saw an American officer with a young civilian woman at his side. I told him that I wanted to speak to him and the woman translated. She was German and the conversation was laborious. The commandant wanted me to tell him all I knew, all I had seen: where the German lines were, what weapons they had, and so on. I told him that I had seen very little. I had heard gunfire from the barn, but whose guns, or what kind they were, I did not know. Had I seen any tanks? I had seen only a partly destroyed one.

Then he told me to go to the school, where the headmaster had been instructed to put up prisoners of war, displaced persons and escapers like me.

While lying in the ditch during the bombing of Nordhausen I had picked up off the ground a 100 mark banknote, which must have been dropped by one of the fleeing civilians. Now I felt all blessings showered upon me. I was free, and even had money. The headmaster led me to a room with hastily arranged beds where I met a French prisoner-of-war who could speak German and with whom I at once made friends. I wanted to smarten myself up a bit and with my 100 marks sought out a barber who realised at once that I was an escaper. He shaved me with trembling hands. They were all wary, the whole village – apprehensive of what was to come; they knew, at least in part, about the Nazi crimes.

When I returned to the school the Frenchman was still there. We decided to visit the American soldiers in their billets, and found them having a meal. They were most hospitable and gave me a giant portion of scrambled egg and white bread – a meal which I had not seen in years.

When we rose next morning the tanks and their crews were gone; our liberators were evidently only an advance party. Were we again in Nazi Germany? The Frenchman and I decided to walk westwards to a place five kilometres away called Keula. On the way we met and were overtaken by numerous jeeps. The soldiers threw us little packets with three cigarettes, some chewing gum and, in some, sweet biscuits.

We spent one night in Keula, being taken care of by the Americans. Now I felt quite safe and next day walked to Mühlhausen in Thuringia which already had a permanent US commandant. I was interviewed in his office by three military men who spoke fluent German – they were probably German refugees who had fled to the USA.

They wanted to listen to my whole story. I told them about my term in prison, about the concentration camps and the clandestine resistance there, not telling them, however, that many in the resistance were Communists.

The Americans were not well briefed on concentration camps but they did know about Buchenwald. They introduced me to the US town commandant who worked in the same room but spoke no German. He summoned the *Bürgermeister* [mayor], who must have been the mayor under the Nazis. He asked me my profession. I replied that I was an electrician. 'Fine,' he said, 'our transformer station has been damaged and you can help us rebuild it.' I smiled at the commandant; he smiled back and ordered the mayor to provide accommodation for me, food and decent clothes. I was put up in an inn and then sought out the clothing depot where I selected a reasonable outfit.

Now, properly dressed, I returned to the inn to treat myself to a warm meal, and found that I had to pay for it and surrender ration coupons, a strange and somewhat baffling procedure after nine years of captivity. I also noticed that dinner guests stopped talking when I entered and stayed more or less silent while I remained there. When I finished the meal the proprietor told me that I had to register with the police.

I found the police station and spoke to an official wearing civilian clothes. He asked my name. I replied, 'Nathan Hirschtritt' (a very Jewish name), and this gave him a shock – apart from being almost completely bald I looked so normal. He stared at me strangely and began filling in a questionnaire. He began with my date of birth, but when he started with other questions I lost my calm and exclaimed, 'Won't you first offer me a chair?'

The official jumped up with fright and left the room. A few minutes later a man wearing a red armband appeared. He asked me who I was and I replied rather briefly. He explained that he himself was an old Buchenwalder, and had been a prisoner for many years. He warned me that we must not now be aggressive or provocative: things must be done calmly. I replied that it was I who was being provoked by an official who sat comfortably at his desk while I had to stand in front of him. The Buchenwalder also informed me of a repatriation camp functioning in the area and directed me to it.

The camp proved to be a huge compound of military barracks. A French guard armed with a pistol stood at the main entrance. After explaining my business I was conducted first to the guardroom and from there to an office where I was questioned by a group of officers of different nationalities. I told them my story but it had to be verified. The fact that I had been a prisoner in concentration camps was not in doubt, but by itself was not sufficient: I could well have been a criminal or a brutal *Kapo*.

The officers called in a few Frenchmen who had themselves been in concentration camps and they interrogated me more closely. I mentioned being in Monowitz and one of the Frenchmen, who had obviously been in the camp, asked me which was my work squad. I replied that I had been a medical orderly in the sick-bay, and he seemed to be satisfied. He must have recognised me; anyhow, he leaned over to the officers and I heard him say, '*C'est un bon camarade.*'

Each barrack of the compound was allotted to a group of prisoners from the same country of origin or form of past captivity – French prisoners of war, French forced labourers, displaced persons, Czechs, Poles, Dutch, and so on. I was placed in the Polish house but wandered from barrack to barrack hoping to find a congenial group to join with or someone I knew. In one of the houses I met a former Soviet officer who explained that Berlin was still not liberated and that I could not be sent there. I entered the 'Dutch house' where people were singing and dancing. An air of gaiety and joy, a spirit of community, of belonging, pervaded the camp. I was affected by it, was happy for them all, and yet remained an outsider.

The next day, 11 April, the news of the liberation of Buchenwald swept the camp and there was general jubilation and delirious joy all round.

The following day I went back to the office and told them of our group's resolution to meet in Paris if separated in flight. The officers nodded in agreement. Lorries with repatriates were leaving constantly. Smiling men were being seen off by their comrades who themselves had for one reason or another to wait longer. All but the Poles were anxious to be next to go, especially the French, Dutch and the Czechs.

My turn came four days later. Our lorry took us to the main railway station in Frankfurt-on-Main, from where normal passenger as well as freight trains were leaving at short intervals for Metz and France. There must have been hundreds of thousands of Frenchmen in Germany during the war who were now returning home. I also boarded one of the freight trucks, but the journey could not be compared with those between concentration camps – we now had adequate food and all necessary amenities.

On reaching the frontier at Thionville we had to filter through a control cordon formed by the French Ministry of the Interior. A file was opened on each of us. I gave my usual story: that I was German, a Berliner of former Polish citizenship, but now stateless. I saw the official marking the top of my file with the word 'Communist' in red.

I was told that I could not be admitted to France, not having been deported from there. Germans, Poles and all others formerly resident in France could return, but I was 'repatriable' to Poland or Germany.

Needless to say, I had no intention of complying and began to think of a way out. Luckily, I remembered that one of the eleven planning to escape with me during the air raid in Nordhausen was a Frenchman, Dr Hofstein, whom I knew well and who had told me that he had a brother who was a dentist in Thionville. It was now very easy to find him; most Thionvillers spoke German and someone I asked knew Hofstein's address. When I met him he was of course anxious to learn all I knew about his brother, his state of health, chances of successful escape and survival.

I was rather pessimistic about the fate of recaptured prisoners after an attempted escape but was not sure that his brother had in fact been recaptured by the SS. Moreover, I did not want to deprive Hofstein of the hope of his brother remaining alive and spoke rather more reassuringly than I really felt.

My own problem of getting to Paris was resolved easily. Hofstein called the nurse from the consulting room and asked her to accompany me in a roundabout way to Metz railway station four kilometres away. This she did, on her bicycle. I walked at her side and we soon reached the station where I boarded a repatriation train for Paris.

In Paris we were taken to the Hotel Lutétia which was the headquarters of the Gestapo during the occupation and was now used by repatriates. I was given a bed and, leaving my few possessions on it, went down to the reception around which stood a number of men with tricolour armbands – members of the French resistance. I told them who I was and that I wanted to talk to someone from the Communist newspaper, the *L'Humanité*. They told me how to get there and I found a journalist who spoke German and with whom I sat for five hours recounting my experiences. He took it all down and introduced me to the editor, Marcel Cachin.

I also wanted to meet German comrades. The German Communist Party as such did not function in France at the time but there existed an organisation of German anti-fascists with a central office in Paris. The *L'Humanité* journalists gave me its address and notified it of my coming. I was interviewed there by three comrades, former International Brigaders – Willi Kreikemeyer, Adolf Pöffel and Fritz Hilger – who asked me to write a detailed autobiography and then return for further conversation. This I did. Later I maintained contact with another German International Brigader and well known member of the French resistance, Max Friedemann.

When I returned to the hotel I found that my bed had been occupied by two men. I explained that I had slept in it the previous night. However, they were plainly irritated by my German and were anxious to see the back of me. I was then told by the reception that I had to move: the hotel was overfull, and I was advised to go to the Jewish Community Shelter for the Homeless.

The manageress of the shelter, Sarah Kuttner, was a member of the French Communist Party and I got on well with her. I was given a bed and soon met there some of those who had been with me in one or other of the concentration camps.

After a few days we decided to form a sort of informal committee which I chaired. One of our activities was to vet applicants for help. This proved useful. We were able to spot a man who had been a soldier in Vlasov's collaborationist anti-Soviet army, another who betrayed a French comrade to the SS and one who had been a brutal *Kapo* beating prisoners in his work-squad.

Everywhere people were looking for their deported and missing relatives. Many came to us with their inquiries and we tried to help. Some people looked at me with a certain suspicion: how had I survived nine years of imprisonment when ninety-nine of every hundred perished? I was often asked this and pondered over it. An element of luck can certainly not be ignored. However, I believe we survived mainly thanks to the help given by our comrades, and I would stress particularly the help given to Jews by their non-Jewish comrades; not only by such heroic personalities as Ludwig Wörl or Ernst Schneller, who I have mentioned here, but also by many others who at greatly increased risk to themselves helped their even more exposed and vulnerable Jewish comrades. We were indeed a band of brothers.

Occasionally, though all too seldom, we were informed of happy reunions. I also tried to find members of my family, and after two months received a letter from my sister, Helen, in England. My letter in reply is reproduced as the Prologue to this book.

My sister tried hard to obtain permission for me to come and stay with her. Entry to the UK was at the time greatly restricted but she had a friend, John Platts-Mills, who was a Member of Parliament, and he showed a copy of my letter to the Home Secretary, Herbert Morrison. As a result I was given permission to stay three months with my sister in a house, which she shared with a friend, near Semer, in the lovely county of Suffolk.

Those months were perhaps the happiest time of my life. Endless talks with my sister and friends, walks in the country, playing with the children; life was full of joy. Neighbours and friends heard of the erstwhile prisoner of the Nazis staying in their midst and came to see us bringing me part of their rationed eggs, butter and milk. This was a new and most moving experience; I shall never forget their kindness and generosity. **"**

12
Afterword

Jonny's course after his return to Berlin was not all plain sailing. He ran into both doldrums and heavy weather, but this is another story. Some of his work was, however, connected with his experience in the concentration camps. He assisted in the planning and building of the Sachsenhausen memorial exhibition and was a member of the Auschwitz Committee, whose aim is to record all that happened in that camp and to bring to justice those responsible for the crimes committed in it.

He met and later married Margarete (Gretl) Neumann, a former member of the *Rotes Sprachrohr*. They had a daughter and two granddaughters, the eldest of whom, in Jonny's own proud words, 'plays the guitar better than I ever did' and hopes to become a professional musician.

Loved by all who knew him, and having been awarded some of his country's highest honours, Jonny Hüttner died suddenly and without pain, from heart failure, in October 1987.

Part Two:
Red Megaphones

13
Margarete Berndt

In 1933, when members of the *Rotes Sprachrohr* were joining other dramatic societies in order to be able to exert some influence, Gretl was advised by Maxim Vallentin not to do so because she was too well known and could alert the Gestapo to the clandestine activities of the company.

The SA came one day to fetch her. Fortunately she was out, could be warned by her sister, and went into hiding with an aunt in Neukölln, a district of west Berlin. On another occasion she was summoned and questioned by the Gestapo. They had in front of them a form she had once filled in on joining the Workers' Theatre League. They asked her about her political views and activities. She replied that her only interest was being on the stage, what was said was of no great concern to her. Her 'misdeed', having in any case been committed in the past, before the Nazis came to power, they let her go.

She was for a time still a member of the Pankow group of the *Rotes Sprachrohr* but eventually lost all contact with the Communist Party – like many thousands of former party members – and was left to her own devices.

She worked in the Osram Telefunken factory and kept a battery radio set in the home her family had built on a north Berlin allotment site, listened to the BBC and shared the news with some members of her family and a few trusted colleagues at the factory. Moscow broadcasts were very heavily jammed but she once heard Maxim Vallentin reading

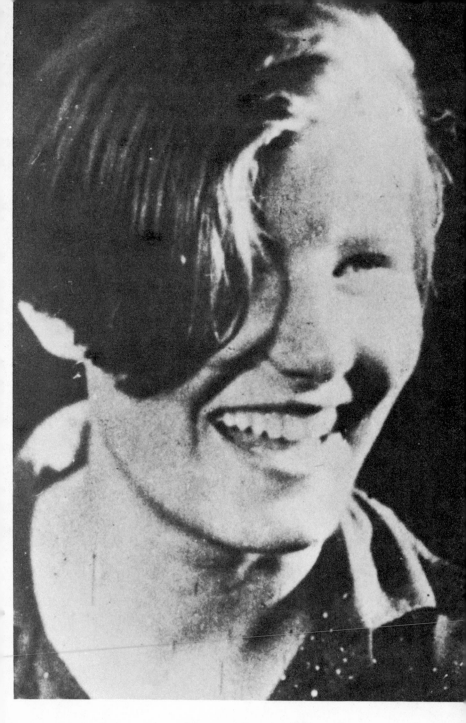

Margarete Berndt in 1931

letters written by German prisoners of war to their families, as well as those written by the wives to the soldiers asking for various 'gifts' from Russia. When Soviet troops entered her part of Berlin she organised some of the residents to clear the streets with her for the army, and arranged the equitable distribution of available resources and accommodation. She rejoined the Communist Party, worked in party offices and was a delegate to the 1946 congress at which the two working-class parties joined to form the SED – the Socialist Unity Party of Germany.

In 1939 she had married another former member of *Rotes Sprachrohr*, Max Neumann. He was called up, served in the Wehrmacht and was captured in Russia. The last of his letters came in 1946; then she heard no more from or about him and assumed that he had died.

In 1948 she met Jonny Hüttner, whom she knew from the *Rotes Sprachrohr* days, and they soon started living together. Their daughter was born in 1950 but they could not formally marry till 1951 when the presumed death of Max Neumann was officially accepted.

14

Helen Hüttner

One morning, in the winter of 1933-34, Mike (Erich Mirek) did not turn up at a rendezvous he had arranged with Helen and she cycled, as she often had done, to his home. No one was in and she went down to the boilerhouse to look for Mike's father, one of whose duties it was to take care of the boiler. On entering she found herself facing two uniformed policemen. She asked for Herr Mirek and then, when she tried to turn back, the policemen stopped her. They had arrested Mike and were now waiting for his father. She was being held to prevent her from warning him. Apart from that the police were friendly, joked, and, since the waiting lasted hours, shared their sandwiches with her. She decided to join in the banter. At one point one of them put his helmet on Helen's head to see 'what she would look like as a policeman', and that very moment the door opened and one of the *Rotes Sprachrohr* members, Ala Löw-Beer, walked in. Astonished as she was at the scene, she yet had the presence of mind to ask calmly if Frau so and so lived in the house. Helen said that the porter was out and then darted after her exclaiming, 'Wait, you could try next door!' and, before the policemen pulled her back, whispered: 'Mike arrested. See you at ...'

When in the end the police let her go she found Ala who gave her a message from the Vallentins. She and Gerda Sandberg were to join the Vallentins in Prague because both were Jewish and thus in danger. Since Mike was now under arrest and the Gestapo might know or could find out about their relationship, Helen decided not to return home and

Gerda thought that she could stay the night at her aunt's. The latter agreed, and put Helen up in her young son's bed, a choirmaster, who was that evening practising with his choir. On returning, he found his bed occupied, and next morning when told that his 'guest' was on the run, gave her a few marks to help her on her way. (Fifty years later Helen and her husband went to the Albert Hall in London for a concert given by the Dresden Philharmonic Orchestra, conducted by Kurt Sanderling. The programme notes mentioned that he had been a refugee at Leningrad, where he studied conducting under Mravinsky, and had become, before returning to the German Democratic Republic, conductor of one of the great Soviet orchestras – the Leningrad Philharmonic. Helen thought that he might well be the youth whose bed she used on her escape, and so in the interval she and her husband went behind the platform to the dressing rooms, and, threading their way past the crowded musicians, stepping over the cello and double-bass cases, found Sanderling. 'Were you the boy in whose bed I slept that night ...?' Helen asked. Yes, he was; he remembered it well. 'Well then,' Helen's husband said, 'we still owe you three marks fifty.' 'No, four marks,' came the reply, 'and it was my last pocket money!')

Gerda and Helen went off next day, and crossed the mountains forming the Czech-German frontiere on foot, walking over snowed up or icy paths, but this route was often used by Communist Party couriers and they had an experienced guide to help them. On reaching Prague they stayed at first with the Vallentins, who lived in a room with a double bed in which all four of them had to sleep. Later, the four found an unfurnished flat consisting of a room and kitchen, where Helen slept with Gerda. Before the projected agitprop company came into being the Vallentins left for the USSR, and the project was taken over by Gerda Sandberg.

Helen stayed in Prague over a year and remembers her mixed feelings during that time: the sadness of leaving home, family and the imprisoned Mike, the discomforts of life as a refugee ... They were not allowed to take up employment and Helen had to be content with a few moonlighting jobs, such as teaching German. They lived mainly on bread and dripping, the accommodation was dismal, bed bugs ubiquitous. But the city was beautiful, the Czech comrades were, unlike the Germans, easy-going and friendly, and often invited the exiles to share their frugal meals. Life was exciting. There were many artists, writers and other intellectuals among the refugees and it was easy for Helen to mix with them.

Early in 1935 she was sent to a Communist Party school in the mountains, which was also attended by friends from Berlin, including Mike, now free again, and her brother Jonny. Jonny spoke of their clandestine work in Berlin. In his view it was possible for her to return. She herself felt that the place for a Communist, if not forbiddingly exposed, was Germany, and decided to return. So, in the summer of 1935, her first stay in Czechoslovakia came to an end.

In Berlin she resumed membership of the clandestine Prenzlauer Berg group. Unemployment had eased and she found work as a wages clerk in a small factory where Jonny was also employed as a delivery man. Relations with Mike were complicated. He was not a Jew, and if their liaison were discovered not only would they themselves be severely punished but their comrades would be also endangered. Moreover, Mike was in another group – in Neukölln – and they could meet only rarely and secretly: in the country, in cinemas and in trustworthy friends' homes. Hence they went on deciding to separate, and would kiss and say good-bye with tears in their eyes, only to fall into each other arms again. Love proved stronger than the Nürnberg laws.

Two rules of conspiracy were invariably enforced. One was to know as little as possible about the activity of a comrade. Thus Helen did not know and never asked what Mike did for the party and vice versa. The second was that when groups or a few individuals met, the first point on the 'agenda' was to decide on what to say if apprehended and asked how they had met each other and what they were now doing together. On the night of their arrest on March 1936 they resolved to say that Trude Seidel and Helen had met in the market-place and that they were now only having a chat and a coffee. They all stuck to this story throughout, and the Gestapo were not able to catch them out in any inconsistency.

At the Alexanderplatz prison Helen waited a week for her first interrogation. This was her most trying period. She had no idea what she would be charged with nor how long they would keep her in solitary confinement. It would be more serious if the Gestapo were to find out that she had been in Prague; they could then accuse her of espionage. However, when the interrogation started she realised that all they knew was that she was Jonny's sister, and that Jonny himself was telling them nothing of any consequence. She acted the naive and totally innocent Jewish girl. When asked if they had talked politics at the Seidels' flat, she queried, 'You mean if butter got dearer?' Her society was the Jewish sports club *Bar Kochba*, and she intended, if she could, to marry and emigrate to Palestine. They threatened to beat her if she did not give them the names of Jonny's friends or tell them more about the Seidels but they did not do so, although on one occasion she was kept twenty-four hours in the interrogation room. Solitary confinement, with nothing to do or read, was increasingly wearisome for a lively young girl, and she began to wish to be formally charged and transferred to a remand prison. At that point she found on one of the walls a graffito which renewed her morale: *Verliert nicht den Mut, Genossen, Gesinnung fordert Opfer* ('Don't lose courage, comrades. Principles demand sacrifice').

One day, towards the end of her imprisonment, the door opened and a Jewish girl was pushed into the cell. The prison was so overcrowded that they could not always enforce isolation. The newcomer, Lola (now Lola Strüwe), had served two and a half years for 'preparation of high treason' and was about to be released. She was an experienced prisoner and, as they both assumed that Helen would also be convicted, Lola taught her prison ruses and how to remain fit with exercises and daily cold water rub-downs of the whole body. They talked and sang; Helen had always been a living anthology of folk songs.

Prison food was terrible – bread and a coffee substitute in the morning and at night, with a thin soup at midday. A few pieces of bacon floated on top of the soup and the girls longed for at least one of them to get into their bowls. It never did: the criminal trusties doling out the soup had their own clients. One day – it was Helen's twenty-first birthday – Lola was at last lucky enough to get a piece of bacon in her soup. She asked Helen to shut her eyes and a moment later the bacon was swimming in Helen's bowl, a birthday present she never forgot. Moreover, after her release Lola returned to the prison gate with a bar of soap and asked the dreaded police to give it to Helen – an act of courage and true friendship.

After seven weeks a Gestapo man came into the cell and ordered, 'Pack your things. You are being released.' The 'things' she had were the soap and a nighty, and these kept dropping out of her hands as in great agitation she tried to wrap something round them. The release was quite unexpected. She was led to an office to sign a statement that she would not divulge anything she had heard or seen in prison. Despite her extreme excitement she forced herself to read through the print carefully before signing. The Gestapo was known sometimes to include in the text an undertaking by the prisoner to co-operate with them. Had she signed this, even without the slightest intention of keeping to it, the Communist Party would not have readmitted her to its ranks.

On leaving prison she thought that the Gestapo would trail her, and decided that her best course was to get home and then vanish before any contact could be made with her by friends or comrades. She had an address where she might find shelter and sent her younger brother to ask if it was still available. It was, and so after two hours she left with only her handbag and, making sure of not being followed, reached the safe house. Her brother brought her luggage later. With her still valid Polish passport she reached Prague without undue difficulty.

In Prague, utterly dejected, Helen walked away from the station. Her brother and the Seidels were in prison, her mother was left in sorrow over the children without any certain means of support. Helen was free but did not know to whom to turn. In this state, crying, she shuffled towards the centrally situated Wenceslas Square, and there walking towards her was Lola. With tears streaming down her face she embraced her friend and was soon led to the German Communist Party's offices, where accommodation was found for her. After debriefing by the party security officials she became once more a *bona fide* refugee and party member.

This time her stay in Czechoslovakia ended after the conclusion of the Munich agreement and the entry of the German troops into the Sudetenland. Occupation of the whole country and the imminence of war were now certain, and arrangements were taken in hand for renewed emigration.

Helen was fortunate in obtaining a British visa, formally for taking up employment as a domestic servant. She left with the last legal transport out of Prague and travelled via Poland and Sweden. She did in fact work at first as a parlour maid in a large country mansion and lived later in a refugee hostel in Wimbledon maintained by the Czech Refugee Trust Fund. There she ran a choir – a small agitprop group which performed at events organised to raise money for their comrades interned on the Isle of Man. She soon married – a doctor (the author), who looked after the refugees – and became a British subject.

15
Erich Mirek

On leaving school in 1927, Erich, or Mike, worked at first as an errand boy but with the help of one of his father's friends found an apprenticeship as a motor mechanic. He was also heavily engaged politically. After the *Roter Frontkämpferbund* (Red Front Line Fighters' League) was banned, another organisation the *Antifaschistische Junge Garde* (the Anti-Fascist Young Guards) took its place in 1928, and Mike was asked by the Young Communist League to be one of its leaders in Wilmersdorf. It was a partly uniformed body: the members wore a black or blue shirt with a red tie, a somewhat military type of belt, a hammer and sickle badge and a cap resembling one usually worn by Ernst Thälmann. Soon this organisation was also proscribed and a protest meeting was arranged with Walter Husemann as the main speaker.[1] Actually, the meeting was never held: the police stopped Mike and Husemann at the entrance to the hall, took them to the police station and kept them there twenty-four hours. Walter Husemann was later to play an important part in Mike's life.

After the Nazis seized power Mike and the Vallentins joined an amateur dramatic society, but they were too well known and thus too vulnerable. The Vallentins were living illegally, knew that the police were already after them, and so it was decided that they should leave the country. Mike guided them and, later, Elli Schliesser across the Riesengebirge mountains into Czechoslovakia. He himself joined a Berlin ramblers' club.

Early one November morning in 1933 the Gestapo and SS broke into the Mireks' flat. They were looking for someone who was no longer there and on searching the flat found anti-Nazi leaflets published by Hans Otto hidden in one of Mike's school atlases.[2] They arrested him and his mother.

Mike was handed over to the Gestapo who interrogated him in their Prinz Albrecht Strasse headquarters. This building was completely sound-proofed and thus immersed in tomblike silence: one heard neither the cries of prisoners nor the sound of the warders' boots. After being severely beaten Mike was asked for the name of the person who gave him the leaflets. He gave them names of people who he knew were no longer in the country. The Gestapo checked this and appeared to be satisfied. He was then transferred to the Columbia House – an old military prison. There he was kept alone in a cell, but later they needed someone to help the plumber lay pipes and picked on Mike. The chief warder told him that some prisoners were being sent to the Oranienburg concentration camp and asked whether he would like to go with them. He added that if Mike stayed he would remain in solitary confinement while by going he would be joining other political prisoners. Since he had no clear idea of what Oranienburg was, and, moreover, was treated abominably by the plumber, he opted for Oranienburg.

In the lorry he sat next to von Papen, a nephew of the former German Reich Chancellor, who had got into trouble through making a derogatory remark about Julius Streicher and his newspaper, *Der Stürmer*. In the courtyard of the old brewery, now used as the concentration camp, they were met by an SA man nicknamed after the NCO in Remarque's novel *All Quiet on the Western Front* – Himmelstoss. He faced Mike and shouted, 'We have long been waiting for you!' Mike's spirits sank, but Himmelstoss squinted badly: the greeting was meant for Mike's neighbour.

Oranienburg held about 3,000 prisoners at the time and conditions were frightful. Prisoners taken for interrogation were often beaten to death and their bodies simply thrown out. Jews were tortured and taunted in every possible way. A new party of prisoners arrived in the early summer of 1934. They were brought from other concentration camps and prisons. Among them was the well known anti-fascist Erich Mühsam.[3] He was in a terrible state, hardly able to stand or move and almost totally deaf – the Nazis had smashed both his ear passages. They continued to torment him in Oranienburg helped by one of the criminal prisoners, who in the previous camp would make Mühsam stand with his mouth open and then spit into it. Mühsam told the comrades that bad as things were they would get still worse when the SS took over from the SA. And so it was. A detachment of the SS arrived from Dachau and one of their first acts was to hang Mühsam.

One day someone noticed von Papen with another prisoner fondling each other under the shower and reported this to the chief of the SA. The latter announced that he was leaving retribution for this 'disgusting act' to the prisoners themselves. Mike with some comrades had by that time formed a well-functioning Young Communist League resistance group in the camp and they took the matter into their own hands. Noting the exact position of Mühsam's tormentor's bunk, they stalked up to it in the middle of the night and settled accounts with him. Von Papen and his friend were left untouched.

Mike was released after six months. Before he left, a group of prisoners arrived from one of the concentration camps in the marshes bringing with them the 'peat-bog soldiers' song' (*Wir sind die Moorsoldaten*). Soon after release Mike went for a visit to Czechoslovakia and taught the song to the comrades there. It soon spread all over that country, indeed all over the world: it became and remains the best known of the concentration camp songs.[4]

In Berlin Mike at once resumed membership of the clandestine Neukölln group of the *Rotes Sprachrohr*. His main problem was now employment: not finding work but keeping it. Every time he had a job the Gestapo would after a month or so inform the employer of his status and that meant instant dismissal. Once he kept a job the whole of nine months – at the Daimler-Benz works outside Berlin – and thought that his employment troubles might be over, but the Gestapo caught up with him. He was called to the office and was told to leave at once. He was not even allowed to collect his tools and clothes. Mike was also dismissed when the Gestapo intervened after he had served for a short spell with the Wehrmacht. He did however pass the journeyman tests of his trade and became a qualified motor mechanic. It was obvious to him that preparations for war were proceeding apace and he got into the habit of discussing his observations with Walter Husemann.

In 1938 he met a girl, Lucie, whom he knew from his early days in the movement. She had been an office worker in the Communist Youth League central office and was transferred for similar work in Moscow. After her return in 1933 she was arrested, served a term of three years in prison and was then taken to Ravensbrück concentration camp. When finally released she remained under police supervision and had to report to them every week, but was told that the supervision would be lifted if she married. Lucie and Mike therefore decided on a political marriage of convenience. For a man, himself on the Gestapo files, to marry someone with Lucie's past in the Germany of 1938 was an act of courage and solidarity. They never lived together, never had a home. Later, during the war, Mike did not want to end the rather fictitious marriage because Lucie would have been entitled to a small pension if he were killed. They agreed on a divorce when Mike returned to Berlin after the war.

Mike was called up for short periods of service with the Wehrmacht when the Germans invaded Austria and then Czechoslovakia. He became a soldier again on the first day of the war in 1939. Most of the time he served as driver or motor mechanic. During the campaign in the Low Countries and France he drove a general of an infantry division or, rather, the general drove himself and Mike followed somewhere in the rear in another car with the general's suitcases. As a general's driver he became automatically a *Feldwebel* (sergeant). He worked later in the motor repair shop of the division where one of his duties was to search for spare parts, which allowed him uncommon freedom of movement. After the French campaign the division was moved to Poland and stationed close to the Soviet frontier on the River Bug. Mike could scarcely accept that war against the USSR was imminent, but when in Berlin he discussed this eventuality with Husemann. He did not know of course that the latter had links with an intelligence-gathering organisation but realised that the information he was bringing was welcome and useful.

On 22 June 1941 Mike's division was one of the first to cross the River Bug and advanced rapidly past Brest into the Pripet marshes where they had to leave their motor vehicles and proceed on foot. The vehicles followed by circuitous roads.

The vehicles lay for some weeks in and around the town of Pinsk. Here Mike made friends with a Jewish girl, a member of the *Komsomol* (Young Communist League), and her family. He had to go on duty to Warsaw and one of the girl's friends asked him to take along food for her parents. Driving towards their address he came up against a wall: his van was standing outside the Warsaw ghetto. German soldiers were allowed in but were forbidden to alight or turn off the main street. He found the address. A crowd stood at the entrance to the house and he asked for the people he was looking for. A woman answered that it was her family. She and the others were terrified – a German NCO coming for them. He went up to their flat with the food. The scene that followed can hardly be described. The people fell all over him, tried to kiss his hands. He had to tear himself away and be gone as soon as possible.

On returning to Pinsk Mike was astonished to hear and scarcely believed that the SS had begun to shoot all Jews. They murdered more than 8,000 in the course of a few days, about 3,000 on the first day, among them his friend's brother. The following day he drove out of town on his motor cycle. Along the road groups of Jews were led by SS men who heaved at them with rifle butts, first on one side then on the other to pack them as close as possible to one another. Then they turned them off the road and simply shot them. The next group had first to carry away the corpses and cover them with a layer of earth before being shot themselves. Mike stopped and took photographs of the scene, a highly dangerous act, as he would certainly have been shot if noticed. He had the film developed and printed in a Warsaw shop and when next in Berlin delivered both film and prints to Husemann, who assured him that the information would be passed on along the right channels.

Erich Mirek's photograph of murdered Jews outside Pinsk in the summer of 1941; members of the SS are visible on the left

This material was probably the first documentary evidence of Nazi atrocities in the USSR. (After the war Husemann's widow found the prints and they were published in the *Berliner Zeitung* – another dangerous step, since Mike could have been suspected of being an accomplice of the murderers.) In the following days Mike tried to rescue some of the people. Some civilians were being employed in their motor workshop and he asked the SS for certain individuals who, he said, were needed in the workshop.

He recalls that some SS officers found a skilled Jewish cobbler and had him make new boots for them. When the boots were ready the officers put the man against the wall and shot him. Mike spoke indignantly about this with his mates in the workshop and was surprised that none disapproved of the officers' action; anti-Semitism had struck deep and wide roots in the German people. Before leaving Pinsk Mike advised his Jewish friends and workmen to disappear in the forests and helped some of them to make their way there.

After the German defeat before Moscow the division was stationed in the town of Orel and Mike renewed contacts with Soviet civilians. He found them very depressed by the deep retreat of the Soviet army and was surprised by their ambiguous attitude to Stalin.

In the spring of 1942 Mike fell ill with infectious hepatitis and was evacuated to Berlin. On returning to the front he was posted as driver to a brigade of self-propelled guns and went with them for a time to the Leningrad front. His company was then withdrawn and sent to France to be formed into a brigade. They were then transported diagonally across Europe to Romania and after a long retreat met the end of the war in lower Austria.

Mike and three of his mates went off by themselves. Still in uniform, they were in danger of being interned as prisoners of war by the Americans and so avoided towns and villages, keeping to the woods, fields and country lanes. Footsore and mostly very hungry their spirits were yet well aloft. They were at last rid of the army, the endless saluting, the constant orders and unconditional obedience. They sang happily as they covered the 350 kilometres to upper Bavaria.

In a small village there one of Mike's companion's family kept a small pub and also had a little land. They treated Mike like their second son and he stayed with them for six months. He hewed wood, repaired bicycles for people in the village, rigged up a still with copper tubes extracted from broken down cars and distilled elderberry schnapps.

Getting back to Berlin was difficult. He had to cross the Soviet zone without valid papers but in the end succeeded in doing so. He stayed for a while with his parents in Wilmersdorf but since he had always hoped to be an actor and work with Maxim Vallentin, contacted and then joined him in Weimar. The Vallentins had formed a drama department in the Weimar Musikhochschule (conservatorium) but met with a number of difficulties. One was that some of the academics were rather reactionary and did not share Maxim's views on training nor his enthusiasm for the Stanislavsky method of acting. Another problem was that the students were all young, and had grown up in Nazi Germany. There were no Communists or Socialists among them. Mike's presence, and his subsequent election to the leadership of the students' council, was therefore invaluable. Later, the town authorities placed the Belvedere castle on the outskirts of Weimar at the disposal of the school. Scenically the castle was perfect but structurally it was of the seventeenth rather than the twentieth century. Much work had to be done to make it habitable. Students had to help – not always willingly. After five years a new company was formed, which, after a tour of the German Democratic Republic, constituted the nucleus of the Maxim Gorky Theatre in Berlin. Mike married one of the school secretaries and remained an actor with the theatre until his retirement.

Notes

1. Walter Husemann, an instrument maker, was a Young Communist League official and journalist. He was imprisoned for two years in Sachsenhausen and Buchenwald (1936-38) and when released linked up with the Schulze-Boysen/Harnack resistance organisation (*Rote Kapelle* or Red Orchestra). He was arrested with many other members of that group in September 1942 and executed on 13 May 1943.
2. Hans Otto, born 1900, was a talented and well known actor, a Communist, and one of the leaders of the Workers' Theatre League. The

SA carried him off in November 1933 to one of their barracks, where he was tortured and then thrown off the roof of the building. He sustained fractures of the skull from which he died a few days later. (Otto Ulrich, the Communist actor in Klaus Mann's *Mephisto*, was in part based on Hans Otto.)

3. Erich Mühsam, born 1878, began writing against German teachers' brutality while still a pupil and was as a result expelled from school. As a young man he joined a group of anarchist writers and was very active in opposition to the First World War. He took an active part in the short-lived Bavarian revolutionary government in April 1919, and when it collapsed was sentenced to fifteen years. Amnestied in 1924 he worked thereafter as an anti-fascist writer, satirical poet, playwright and journalist. He was arrested again on the day of the Reichstag fire and after several transfers was hanged on 11 June 1934.

4. The song was first published in Wolfgang Langhoff's book *Die Moorsoldaten*, one of the first reports on the concentration camps – it appeared in late 1934 or early 1935 in Switzerland. Rudi Goguel, a young Communist from Baden, who later became a historian in the German Democratic Republic, wrote the song in the Börgermoor camp.

16

Elli Schliesser

Elli emigrated in the autumn of 1933, and in 1935 was one of the co-founders, with Maxim Vallentin, of the Hans Otto Club, named after the German actor killed by the Nazis, which brought together German *émigré* actors and anti-fascists in the German-speaking Prague theatre.

Later, probably in 1938, she moved to Paris. After the German occupation she was one of those in the underground engaged in propaganda amongst German soldiers. She was arrested in Paris 1940 and taken to Ravensbrück from where she was transferred to Auschwitz.

While in Paris she had been able to study chemistry and was thus employed on experimental work at Auschwitz – trying to cultivate the kok-saghys plant. In Auschwitz she became one of the resistance leaders. Survivors speak with utmost respect and admiration of her conduct in the camp. She was also greatly interested in cultural work, particularly with German-speaking young women. Her reading of Goethe's *Faust*, much of which she knew by heart, left a lasting impression on all her listeners. For a time she was in serious danger. Her health was bad, she suffered from abscesses of the legs and was sent at one stage to the penal company. In January 1945 she was evacuated with the rest of the camp to Ravensbrück. When the Soviet Army approached, the prisoners were set marching to other destinations. She tried to escape, was caught and nearly executed. She tried again and succeeded at her fourth attempt, by hiding in a camp for French civilian workers and remaining there until the arrival of the Soviet Army.

Elli Schliesser in 1945

After the war she lived for a while in Dresden, where the Soviet administration entrusted her, alongside Hermann Matern, a leading Communist Party official, with the preparation and organisation of the first large anti-Nazi meeting after the liberation.

Later she rejoined the Vallentins and spent a whole night with them recounting all that had happened to her since they parted. Maxim wanted her to work with him in Weimar, where he was forming a new theatre. However, the years of persecution had left unhealed wounds on Elli's mind. The country to which she returned after liberation was painfully disappointing to her. She could neither understand nor accept the German mentality, not only that of the petty bourgeois but even of the workers.

In a letter she wrote in May 1945 to a friend in Paris she quoted Heinrich Heine.

Oh, once I had a lovely fatherland.
    The oaks grew tall.
Up to the sky, the gentle violets swayed.
    I dreamt it all.
I felt a German kiss, heard German words
    (Hard to recall
How good they rang) – the words *Ich liebe dich*!
    I dreamt it all.

She added that she had lost her country not in 1933, when Hitler came to power; *her* country had turned into a dream when she returned after liberation. Eventually she became paranoid, imagining that the SS were all around her. When a car sent by Maxim Vallentin came to collect her one day, she began to scream that the Gestapo had come. After a few weeks in a mental hospital, she set fire to herself and died a few days later. She was thirty-six years old.

17

Gertrud Seidel

Gertrud (or Trude) Knopp joined the *Rotes Sprachrohr* shortly before the Nazi seizure of power, and in December 1933 was arrested by plain-clothes police for trying to collect and send money to the Vallentins in Prague. She was held until March 1934 at the Alexanderplatz police headquarters. Later in 1934 she and Rudolf Seidel were married.

In 1934 and 1935 courses on underground work were organised for groups of Communist Party workers, including members of the *Rotes Sprachrohr*. Trude was sent on such a course held in a mountain hut on the Czech side of the German frontier. Each course lasted a fortnight and participants followed each other in groups pretending to be skiers. Oddly enough the hut was the property of a well known Sudeten German Nazi, who also owned a nearby hotel. He naturally had no idea who the 'skiers' were.

After her arrest with other members of the *Rotes Sprachrohr* in March 1936, Trude was taken first to Alexanderplatz and then to the Moabit remand prison where she was kept for eleven months. She was tried but was acquitted 'for lack of evidence', and worked subsequently as an X-ray technician in a hospital.

She recalls that one day their hospital dentist was missing. After a few days she asked where he was, and was told that he had asked one of his patients to open his mouth, adding the words, 'No, no, wider, wider – like Goebbels.' His assistant had denounced him and next day he was in a concentration camp. This story had a happy end: the dentist survived and opened the first dental surgery in Berlin after the war.

Trude later worked for a doctor, who was a member of the SS, in Berlin's Kurfürstendamm. He once asked her why she never spoke of her husband (Rudi was in Brandenburg prison). 'Unfortunately', she replied, 'I am not allowed to disclose his whereabouts.' The doctor nodded, and assumed that her husband was a member of the 'Kondor Legion' – a German air force formation which was at the time fighting on the side of Franco in the Spanish Civil War. He replied most respectfully, 'Ah, yes – I understand,' and thereafter treated her – a true, faithful German soldier's wife – with greater sympathy and consideration.

Towards the end of the war, when Berlin was being heavily bombed, Trude and her daughter Ursel, born in 1940, were evacuated to a village in what is now Poland and, when the front moved farther west, ended up in Schönschornstein in a house occupied by a number of Communist artists who were busy making plans for the renewal of art in the future liberated Germany.

Immediately after the war the Communist Party decided that education and re-education of children was one of the most urgent tasks in Germany, and advised all members thought to be suitable to train as teachers. Trude did so, and became at first a primary school teacher. She started her new career in a class together with her seven-year-old daughter, who was one of the new pupils. She qualified later as a secondary school teacher, specialising in German and history, and also became a school director.

18
Rudolf Seidel

When the Prenzlauer Berg group was arrested in March 1936 Rudi maintained at his interrogation that the gathering at his home had had no political motive: he had merely placed his flat at the disposal of friends. The Gestapo tried hard to get Jonny Hüttner to incriminate Rudi but could not break him and hence never discovered that Rudi or, for that matter, any one paying dues to Jonny, was a member of the *Rotes Sprachrohr*. Nor were any names disclosed to the Gestapo by the other two prisoners: Jonny's sister Helen and Rudi's wife Gertrud. Consequently, when tried a year later, Rudi was given a relatively mild sentence of two years imprisonment, which he served in Brandenburg-Görden.

Having been in prison twice Rudi was classified as *wehrunwürdig* (unworthy of military service) but was called up in 1943 when, after their defeat at Stalingrad, the Nazis began to round up everyone they could: boys, invalids, old men and criminals. Thus, whilst being trained as a medical orderly, Rudi shared a desk with a pick-pocket. He was sent to France to serve with a company using horses for transport. Captured after the Allied Normandy landing in 1944 he ended up in a prisoner of war camp near Manchester. The prisoners were mainly employed on the land but also had to clear bomb sites and repair drains. In the camp they formed an orchestra and a dramatic society which put on such plays as Bernard Shaw's *Pygmalion*, with Rudi playing Higgins. When peace came he tried his best to be sent back to Germany but had no luck till 1947. He finally found his wife and daughter in a partly wrecked Berlin house at seven o'clock one morning when both were getting ready for school. One of his wife's first remarks was: 'Why are you so late in coming? You could have been of more help earlier.'

Rudi thought at first of joining the Vallentins in Weimar where they were raising young actors for a new theatre, and even went there to discuss this with them, but the Communist Party advised him to take up other employment. He became a personnel manager in a factory and later worked in the book trade.

19
Maxim and Edith Vallentin

The Vallentins, who went into hiding immediately after the Nazi takeover in January 1933, continued illegal work until the autumn of that year when they emigrated to Czechoslovakia. For a time an effort was made by them to keep in touch with those remaining in Berlin. They even arranged a substantial get-together, disguised as a skiing expedition in the Czech mountains, but all this did not amount to much.

In Prague, Maxim Vallentin helped a former member of the *Rotes Sprachrohr*, Gerda Sandberg, form and lead a local agitprop company. In May 1935 they left for Moscow. Maxim was for a time director of the German theatres in Dnepropetrovsk and then in Engels, the capital of the German Autonomous Republic. Later, he worked as announcer on the German service of the Moscow radio, and some former members of the *Das rote Sprachrohr* remember the thrill they felt on recognising his voice when they listened secretly to Moscow. In September 1944 he became a member of a commission which under the chairmanship of the well known poet Johannes Becher prepared plans for the renewal of the arts in a liberated Germany. The Vallentins returned to Germany in June 1945 and at once resumed their theatrical and political work. Maxim formed a theatre school in Weimar and was later the founder and director of the Maxim Gorky Theatre in Berlin.

Maxim, Edith and Thoma Vallentin in 1945

Part Three:
Das Rote Sprachrohr Archive

After the Nazi seizure of power in 1933 it was decided to save the *Rotes Sprachrohr*'s archives by taking them to Holland. They were transported secretly as far as Aachen and, pending a further move, were hidden in the attic of a house belonging to the parents of a friend, Dr Hilde Broda (now Nunn May), who emigrated to England in 1938. She dared not leave the material in the house and thereby endanger her mother, and so stopped in Aachen on her way to England and burned the entire archive. The only material which survives is a full text of *Alles für die Sowjetmacht*, some of which is reproduced below.

The list of members of the company is as complete as is possible in the circumstances. When interviewed, members of the *Rotes Sprachrohr* were unable to recall all their former comrades, while a few of those remembered and listed here were perhaps not full members of the company. The membership list and biographical data which follow are, therefore, necessarily incomplete. The *Rotes Sprachrohr* in the course of its existence had more members than most, perhaps any of the agitprop troupes in Germany – up to forty in 1932 when it formed two teams and also ran a company which put on shows for children – and Jonny Hüttner still collected party dues from twenty members immediately prior to his arrest in March 1936. One point is absolutely certain: no member of the company became a Nazi. Some of the male members were of course conscripted into one of the armed forces, here designated generically as the 'Wehrmacht'. This term is used below; it is not to be confused with the SA or SS. Brief biographical data are given for those members of *Das rote Sprachrohr* who have not featured earlier in this book.

20
Members of Das Rote Sprachrohr

Beer, Hermann, worker. No other data available.

Beguin, Heinz, stonemason. Served in the Wehrmacht during the war. Remained in West Berlin where he was active in the trade union movement. Did not rejoin the Communist Party. Deceased.

Berndt (later Neumann, then Hüttner), Margarete, worker.

Blasch, Erich, engineering worker. One of the leaders of the *Rotes Sprachrohr*. Active till 1936. Served in the Wehrmacht during the war. In 1986 was living in West Berlin.

Budach, Erwin, worker. Left the *Rotes Sprachrohr* in 1932 on joining the Communist Party *Abwehr* (security service). Served in the Wehrmacht during the war. Was later Director of a prison in the German Democratic Republic.

Galewski, Lutz, cabinet-maker. Stage manager of the troupe and Vallentin's deputy when the company was on tour. Emigrated to Australia in 1935. No further data available.

Gerbeit, Grete, worker. Left the troupe in 1929. Emigrated to Spain and then England. Deceased.

Gumbel, Fritz, worker. Wrote some of the plays' texts. Believed to have emigrated to the USSR. No further data available.

Hüttner, Johann, worker. Deceased.

Hüttner (later Crome), Helen, office worker.

Jahnke, Erich, worker. Emigrated to England. Returned to the German Democratic Republic in 1946. Worked as a Socialist Unity Party official. Deceased.

Jahnke, Franz, no further data available.

Josef, Mayka, worker. An actress after the war. Deceased.

Kinitz (later Kubik), Gerda, worker. Active in the Pankow group till 1935 when the group dissolved itself. Worked in a factory during the war. In 1986 was living in the German Democratic Republic.

Kubik, Willi, worker. Husband of Gerda. Active till 1935 when the Pankow group, of which he was member, dissolved itself. Killed whilst serving in the Wehrmacht.

Lerbs, Erich, worker. Joined the Communist Party in 1932. Arrested and imprisoned for three months. Served in the Wehrmacht during the war. In 1986 was living in the German Democratic Republic.

Lerbs, Gustav, worker. Served in the Wehrmacht during the war. Was prisoner of war in the USSR. Returned to the German Democratic Republic. Deceased.

Löw-Beer, Ala, student. An active but not acting member of the company. An Austrian citizen expelled from Germany in 1933. Emigrated later to England. In 1986 was living in Austria.

Löw-Beer, Paul, student. Husband of Ala. An active non-acting member of the troupe. An Austrian citizen expelled from Germany in 1933. Emigrated later to England. In 1986 was living in Austria.

Mirek, Erich, motor mechanic.

Neumann, Lucie, saleswoman. Active till the Pankow group dissolved itself in October 1935. Deceased.

Neumann, Max, cabinet-maker. Active till October 1935 when the Pankow group dissolved itself. Served in the Wehrmacht during the war; was a prisoner of war in the USSR where he fell ill and died.

Neumann, Richard, student. A talented pianist. Emigrated in 1933. No further information available.

Neumann, Traudl, office worker. Married a Belgian doing forced labour in Germany and emigrated with him to Belgium after the war.

Poldi (first name unknown), worker. The company's violinist. His father was beaten to death by the SS. His mother was so terrified that he had to give up all political activity. Probably killed serving in the Wehrmacht.

Pollex, Walter, worker. One of the leaders of the company. Served in the Wehrmacht and was killed at Stalingrad.

Sandberg (later Kohlmey), Gerda, office worker. Set to music some of the company's texts and songs. Emigrated to Prague where she formed and ran an agitprop troupe. Later emigrated to England. In 1986 was living in the German Democratic Republic.

Schliesser, Elli, unemployed.

Seidel, Gertrud, X-ray technician.

Seidel, Rudolf, book-keeper.

Spicker, Hans, printing worker. Joined the troupe in 1933. Was leader of the Pankow group till October 1935 when the group dissolved itself. Imprisoned in 1941 with wife and child in the Theresienstadt concentration camp. Later transferred to Auschwitz and then Mauthausen where he was liberated. In 1986 he was working in the Berlin Committee of the Anti-Fascist Resistance Organisation of the German Democratic Republic.

Thilo, Fritz, worker. Active until 1934. Served in the Wehrmacht. In 1986 was living in West Berlin.

Tornseifer, Erna, worker. Father and brother beaten to death by the Nazis. Emigrated to Czechoslovakia, then USSR and England. In 1986 was living in the German Democratic Republic.

Vallentin, Edith, ballet dancer.

Vallentin, Maxim, actor.

Weisenberg, Rudi, electrician. Active till 1936. Served in the Wehrmacht. After the war was a trade union official in West Germany.

Wolter, Martha, worker. Wife of Walter Husemann who was member of the *Rote Kapelle* ('Red Orchestra', the name given by the Nazis to the Schulze-Boysen-Harnack resistance organisation). Arrested with her husband and imprisoned in the Ravensbrück concentration camp. Noticed there by Heinrich Himmler who was so impressed by her beauty, with the features of 'ideal German womanhood', as to order her immediate release. Deceased.

21

'All For Soviet Power'

The show would start with a shrill whistle and drum roll followed by the company's signature song (*Truppenlied*), partly sung and partly spoken by the whole cast. The music was by Hanns Eisler.

Wir sind das Rote Sprachrohr –
Sprachrohr der Massen sind wir –
Wir sprechen aus was euch bedrückt –
Wir sprechen aus was euch befreit!

Wir sind das Rote Sprachrohr –
Sprachrohr des Massen sind wir.
Kein Gott, kein Bonze, kein Minister
frisst aus der Futterkrippe unbestraft –
denn wir posaunen aus, wir stöbern auf –
Wir shcwefeln aus – mit Spott und Ernst,
Wir rufen auf zum Klassenkampf!

Wir sind das Rote Sprachrohr –
Sprachrohr der Massen sind wir!

(We are the Red Megaphone –
The masses' megaphone are we.
We speak of what oppresses you –
We speak of what frees you!

We are the Red Megaphone –
The masses' megaphone are we.
No God, no boss, no minister

Shall feed unpunished from the manger.
We trumpet forth, we dust away,
We sulphurise with earnest speech and ridicule.
We call for class struggle!

We are the Red Megaphone —
The masses' megaphone are we!)

A single actor then stepped forward: 'As you know, the Komsomol invited us to the Soviet Union. There we saw the power of the proletariat and its work — the building of socialism. We promise to mobilise the masses against imperialist war threatening the USSR, and to defend the land of the dictatorship of the proletariat. We promise to defend the masses against imperialist war and to support the Young Communist League in winning over the majority of the working class. This is the contract we entered into with the Leningrad Komsomol Theatre.'
The show concluded with a solemn oath.

Mit dem Fünfjahresplan – für die Sowjetmacht!
So stürmen wir voran – für die Sowjetmacht!
Im Schacht und auf dem Feld – für die Sowjetmacht!
Jetzt bauen wir unsere Welt – für die Sowjetmacht!

Der Bolschewisten Sieg – für die Sowjetmacht!
Ihr langer Bürgerkrieg – für die Sowjetmacht!
Soll uns ein Ansporn sein – für die Sowjetmacht!
Uns selber zu befrein – für die Sowjetmacht!

Des Nachts zum kleben gehn – für die Sowjetmacht!
Kämpft mutig Tag für Tag – für die Sowjetmacht!
Nicht nur im Endgefecht – für die Sowjetmacht!
Im Tageskampf erst recht – für die Sowjeetmacht!.

Das Herz voll Todesmuts – für die Sowjetmacht!
Wir geben unser Blut – für die Sowjetmacht!
Erhebt die Faust zum Schwur – für die Sowjetmacht!
Für rote Diktatur – für die Sowjetmacht!

(With the Five Year Plan – for Soviet power!
We storm on and on – for Soviet power!
In mines and in the fields – for Soviet power!
We are building now our world – for Soviet power!

The story of the Bolsheviks – for Soviet power!
Their lengthy civil war – for Soviet power!
Should be for us a spur – for Soviet power!
To liberate ourselves – for Soviet power!

To stick up posters at night – for Soviet power!
To struggle bravely day by day – for Soviet power!
Not only in the last fight – for Soviet power!
But specially day by day – for Soviet power!

Our hearts free from fear – for Soviet power!
We offer all our blood – for Soviet power!
Raise up your fists to swear – for Soviet power!
For the red dictatorship – for Soviet power!)

The spectators were called to join in the oath and would
stand up with fists raised to do so. They would then disperse
into the night with the songs and the oath still ringing in their
ears.

Index